CW00505426

CHRIST FOR POST-CHRISTIAN EUROPE

R. Peprah-Gyamfi

Thank You Jesus Books

Published by Thank You Jesus Books

www.peprah-gyamfi.org
email: **info@peprah-gyamfi.org**

ISBN: 978-1-913285-28-9

www.peprah-gyamfi.org

Contents

Preface vii

Preamble xi

INTRODUCTION: A Return match of sorts xiii

**PART 1: A brief profile of an unintended
   missionary to Europe** 1
Growing up in a little African village 1
My conversion story 3
Adventure to Europe 12
Disappointed Expectations..16

**PART 2: A brief look at the history of
   European Christianity** 21
Reformation 23
Impact of Christianity on Europe.............................24
European missionary activities 24

PART 3A: The decline of European Christianity........27
Intro 27

**PART 3B: Brief overview of the factors leading
to the decline of European Christianity** 31
Science &Technology: The Big Bang Theory,
 The Theory of Evolution by natural selection as
 postulated by Charles Darwin, Fossil finds by
 palaeontologists 31
Perceived contradictions in the Bible 33
Perceived failings of the established churches
 past and present...33
The politicization of the church 34
Confusion concerning which religion holds the truth............34
The European mindset 35
Catastrophes, sufferings, injustices etc.
 in the face of a loving God 35
Wars past and present..36
Poverty among populations who hold on to Christianity........37
Difficulty coming to terms with the
 concept of Satan, demons, principalities........................37
Humanistic worldview...37
Prosperity and the European Welfare State system................38
Social Media 38
Miscellaneous 38

**PART 3C: A more detailed look at the factors
leading to the decline of European Christianity**............39
Science & Technology: The Big Bang theory,
 The Theory of Evolution, Palaeontology 39
Perceived contradictions in the Bible 46
Perceived failings of the established church
 past and present...48
The politicization of the church 49
Confusion concerning which religion holds the truth 49
The European Mindset..52

Catastrophes, sufferings, injustices, etc.,
 in the face of a loving God..57
Wars past and present 59
Poverty among those worshipping God............................61
Difficulty coming to terms with the
 concept of Satan, demons, principalities.........................62
Humanistic worldview 63
Prosperity and the European Welfare State System.............63
Social Media 65
Miscellaneous 66

PART 4 : Effects of rejection of Christ by Europe 67
Post-Christian Europe like a ship without anchor..................67
Biblical teachings on creation rejected 73
Biblical teachings on sexuality and marriage rejected...........74
Family breakdown 79
Mental Health Crisis 80
Subtle persecution of Christians 85

PART 5: Thoughts and Prayers 87
What then is the way forward? 87
A fervent prayer for European Christian Revival 93

Preface

This comprehensive overview of the extent to which the "sea of faith" has receded almost to the point of drying up in Europe gives a very valuable insight into the present state of spiritual Europe. Superficially a prosperous continent with advanced technology and an abundance of material wealth, a closer look lays bare the spiritual and psychological poverty of the population. This closer look is what our author does so well in this book which appropriately ends with a heartfelt prayer for spiritual healing and revival in Europe.

It was the Victorian poet Matthew Arnold who worked as an inspector of schools, who so clearly saw into the future in his prophetic poem 'Dover Beach', which in 1867 foresaw how the sea of faith would dry up in England—which is also so true of the decline of faith in Europe. Faith would recede like the tide going out, washing over the shale as it exposes the naked shingles of the shore:

> The Sea of Faith
> Was once, too, at the full, and round earth's shore
> Lay like the folds of a bright girdle furled.
> But now I only hear
> Its melancholy, long, withdrawing roar,
> Retreating, to the breath

Of the night-wind, down the vast edges drear
And naked shingles of the world.

Matthew Arnold's near despairing conclusions about the future state of Christianity in Europe is so well captured in this book by a medical doctor educated in Europe and born in a little village in Africa. Europe is like an ailing patient desperate for a re-awakening—for the Gospel of Jesus Christ, once preached by missionaries in Africa and throughout the world, to be preached again in Europe—where ironically the original missionaries came from before the sea of faith retreated.

What Europe needs, our author reveals, is a new mission—a new army of missionaries, to bring back the Gospel to Europe. Unfortunately, even in Africa today, the role of sincere and genuine missionaries who sowed the seeds of the Gospel in a past era is often misunderstood and seen as a form of colonial exploitation. Admittedly Europeans exploited Africa for their own wealth in colonial times, but to throw out the genuine missionaries with the exploiters is surely to throw out the baby with the dirty bathwater. Blaming the missionaries is perhaps an understandable misconception made, for instance, by the much respected and renowned author Ezekiel Mphahlele in his book *The African Image*, where he went so far as to blame the missionaries in Africa for 'hijacking' the indigenous African faith of ancestor worship.

Our author, Dr Peprah-Gyamfi, make some excellent points in this book—especially about the strange phenomenon of the Englishman whose home is his castle and yet accommodates all and sundry with their diverse religions while he allows his own Christian faith to evaporate! But to restore the sea of faith to Europe is a mission we can only applaud, for it is a God-given initiative. As he points out, the Bible contains the core teachings of Christianity that deserve to be re-implanted into Europe. As he says, the Bible can be regarded as the "Christian Constitution" where the core belief of the Gospel is the promise of Jesus Christ to grant eternal life to whoever accepts Him—a mission that needs to be prayerfully directed at an ailing Europe so that all may have new hope and new life.

Charles Muller
MA (Wales), PhD (London), DEd (SA), DLitt (UFS)

Preamble

The other day I watched television footage of pedestrians interviewed on the streets of London concerning their belief in God.

"Do you believe in God?" the interviewer asked passers-by on the open street. The replies ranged from a clear "No" to shades of "No" and "Yes".

The majority of those interviewed replied with an emphatic "No!".

The reasons those who answered with a "no" gave for their stance ranged from total disbelief in the supernatural, skepticism in the supernatural, reasons bordering on the failings of the church, the presence of evil in the world, and so on.

The outcome of the interview did not surprise me.

Indeed, statistics show a good proportion of UK adults do not believe in God. Concerning Christianity, statistics show only 6% of the UK adult population consider themselves "Practicing Christians".

The UK situation reflects the general trend in several other places in Europe. Indeed, Christianity is in decline in several parts of Europe.

The bitter reality is that Europe, the continent that has been exposed to the Christian message more than any other continent, has turned its back on the Christian Gospel.

Yes, right across Europe, the ancient cathedrals and churches which bear witness to the predominant role Christianity played of old on the continent are deserted; some are in ruins while others have been turned into cultural centers, shops, hotels, apartments or even converted to mosques.

Yes, in no other part of the world has Christianity been abandoned the way it has been in Europe. Europe, which sent missionaries to the rest of the world, has sadly abandoned the faith.

European Christianity may well be seen as a patient who has over the years been on admission on a normal hospital ward. Over time its condition has deteriorated to the point which necessitates admission to the ICU.

Now matters have deteriorated even further, to the point where the patient has been placed on life support—where doctors and nurses are desperately fighting to rescue the patient.

Will success crown their efforts?

INTRODUCTION
A Return match of sorts

Whilst a student at the Hanover Medical School in the northern German city in the late 1980s, a group of nurses from Ghana arrived at the medical school on an exchange program.

One day whilst one of them was attending to a patient awaiting surgery, she politely requested to pray for him.

"No, I don't believe in any God!" came his prompt answer. "I have placed my faith in the doctors. They have gone through the requisite training. I trust in their skills and competence to help cure my condition."

"Sir," the nurse replied, "I also trust medical practice; otherwise, I wouldn't be working as a nurse. I do believe, though, in Almighty God. So I don't see any contradiction between medical science and prayer."

"No, you cannot change my mind. I don't believe in any God!"

This reaction of the patient came as a big surprise to the healthcare personnel who had just recently arrived in Europe. When I met the nurse a few days later, she brought up the matter:

"Robert, what is wrong with people here? I thought they spread Christianity to us?" she inquired after narrating her experience.

"Well," I replied, "I thought likewise before coming to Europe. My stay has taught me otherwise."

I took the opportunity to narrate an experience I had during my early days in Germany. Incidentally, it also happened in a hospital setting.

In February 1983, I underwent surgery on my left ankle in a hospital in West Berlin. I took my Bible along with me to the hospital. As is my custom, I read it regularly.

I never realized that what I considered a standard practice would attract someone's attention. A few days after undergoing surgery, Ilse, the physiotherapist assigned to me, seeing me reading my Bible, ventured the following observation:

"I want to confess one thing—since I started working in this hospital several years ago, you are the first patient I have seen reading a Bible!"

"Are you serious?!" I replied, taken aback.

"Well, I am curious to know how long you have lived here. Sadly, few residents in this society wish to be associated with the Bible. Only a few shame themselves to be seen reading the Bible in such a public place!"

"That is a shame!"

"Well, that is the reality. Europe has become a mission field. Indeed, Europe needs people like you to bring back the Gospel of salvation to the population. That indeed is the case."

Now, back to the nurse from Ghana and her unbelieving German patient. The patient, a man in his fifties, left the matter to rest. The friendly nurse from Ghana continued to provide care to the individual but desisted from bringing up the issue of faith in their subsequent interactions.

The Ghanaian nurse could, as it was, count herself blessed. However, there is a case of a nurse in England that made headlines for a similar 'misdemeanor'. Whilst at work, she politely requested to pray for a patient in her care. The patient turned down the request. The roommate of the patient concerned did not leave the matter to rest. Instead, she complained to the hospital authorities, who did not brush aside the complaint. Instead, they suspended the nurse pending further investigation, accusing her, among other things, of "religious harassment." Though she was eventually reinstated to her position, the fact she was suspended just for politely offering to pray for a patient illustrates the dire state of Christianity in the British Isles.

Indeed, whereas I lamented over the state of Christianity in Germany, the situation that met me when I moved to the UK nearly broke my heart! I don't want to exaggerate. Based on my more than a decade and a half stay in the UK, my impression is that Christianity is not only marginalized in the UK; one could run into trouble with an open confession of faith.

As in the case of the nurse cited above, if one dares confess one's faith in the workplace, it could lead to a job loss!

The case of the nurse just cited is not the only one of its kind experienced by Christians in the workplace. There are indeed numerous examples. As expected, not all the cases make it to the headlines.

Another case that made headline news in the UK involved an employee of British Airways (BA). She got into trouble just by wearing a necklace displaying the cross.

Still staying in the UK, I may be wrong in my assessment, but I always tell myself that pub culture and football have replaced Christianity as the prevalent religion in the British Isles. Indeed, in Britain, on Friday evenings, pubs are filled; in many cases people drink themselves crazy and wake up the next day with a hangover!

If they managed to get up early the next day, some who filled the pubs on Friday nights would later head to the football stadium to watch their clubs in action.

And Sunday morning? Will those who filled the pubs and football stadia on Saturday make it to the church on Sunday? Forget it!

What, then, has led Western Europe, in particular, and Europe, in general, to turn their backs on the Gospel of the King of Kings and Lord of Lords? Why has a good proportion—if not the majority—of Europeans rejected the Christian message of Salvation, the Good News of the cross, which offers stability in an unstable world and gives strength to the soul?

Why are the churches empty on Sundays when, on the other hand, the football stadia, pop concerts and other entertainment venues are overbooked?

Why do Europeans flock to the beaches, football stadia, and other Sunday events and leave the churches empty?

Of course, I see nothing wrong with others enjoying their pastimes in good and bad weather. I would nevertheless wish they devoted at least a wee bit of their time to advance the faith of their fathers.

Often, I do ask myself the question:

What does Europe find offensive about the Good News of Salvation?

What do they find offensive about the soothing words of the Lord? Words such as:

"Come unto me all ye that labour and are heavy laden, and I will give you rest."

"I am the good shepherd."

"If the Son sets you free, you will be free indeed."

In this book I will use the insights I gained from my interactions with Europeans, especifically my German and British friends, colleagues, patients, etc., to outline what, in my view, has contributed to Christianity's decline in Europe. I will then touch on how the rejection of the Gospel has affected society.

Finally, in line with the Christian calling, "go into the world and make disciples of all nations", I will politely invite them to "taste and see the goodness of the Lord."

Apart from fulfilling the Christian duty I have just referred to, my undertaking could also be regarded as a payback exercise or a return match for the benefits I received in accepting the Gospel message.

How, indeed, could the Good News of Salvation reach the shores of my native Ghana in particular and Africa in general without the tremendous efforts of European missionaries?

There is indeed an ongoing debate about the role missionaries played in colonising the continent.

"When the missionaries came to Africa, they had the Bible, and we had the land. They said, 'Let us pray.' We closed our eyes. When we opened them, we had the Bible, and they had the land"—to quote the late Kenyan president Jomo Kenyatta

Accepted that the European missionaries to Africa were not angels! They were human with flaws, like anyone else.

Whatever the shortcomings of some among them, their efforts no doubt led to the spread of Christianity on the African continent. I bear a debt of gratitude to their efforts, which eventually, albeit indirectly, led me to faith in the King of Kings and Lord of Lords.

So, I am engaged in a return match of sorts, a payback time in the positive sense. Yes, my undertaking is my way of reimbursing the descendants of the Christian missionaries to Africa, the debt of gratitude I owe to their ancestors for spreading the Good News of the Cross to Africa.

Before I tackle the assignment I have set for myself, I pray to the Loving Father of Heaven and earth for the needed wisdom and insight.

PART 1

A brief profile of an unintended missionary to Europe

Growing up in a little African village

So I am undertaking an assignment with the ultimate goal of helping to rekindle the Christian faith in Europe.

Before I proceed, allow me to pause briefly to give the reader a brief background of myself and how I ended up in Europe.

I was born in a village called Mpintimpi in Ghana. The little settlement is situated about 120 kilometres to the north-west of Accra, Ghana's capital city. The village has, in the meantime, grown a bit in size. When I was growing up, it was so tiny that one of my classmates at primary school used to boast that he could urinate around the whole settlement in one go!

According to my mother, I was born in the small rectangular wooden structure that served as the family bathroom. It measured about one metre in length and eighty centimetres in width. The wooden wall rose to about a metre and a half above ground level. At the top, the structure was open to the free tropical skies. The floor was not cemented but covered with fine gravel.

The makeshift bathroom of the family served as my labour ward. It is superfluous to mention that a professional midwife did not attend to me; an elderly lady of the village who had over the years learnt the art of delivery on her own provided my mother with the needed assistance.

When I finally arrived in the world, I took my first breath and screamed in protest for having been forced to leave the comfortable conditions in my mother's womb for the prevailing tropical heat of Africa!

It is also superfluous to state here that no paediatrician was around to check on me, to ascertain whether everything was okay with me.

No specialist was around to examine me to determine whether all was well with me. In line with the Twi proverb 'God drives away the disturbing flies from the beast deprived of a tail', my parents looked to Providence to take care of their tiny new arrival in the world.

Neither Mama nor Papa attended school. As Papa used to tell us, he had a burning desire to go to school, but his parents did not have the means to enable him to fulfil his childhood dreams.

In one respect, I was more fortunate than my parents.

About the time of my birth, the then Gold Coast gained independence from the British colonial administration and was re-named Ghana.

The government of the newly independent country introduced free and compulsory education. Woe unto anyone who refused to take a child of school-going age to school!

I started going to school when I was about six years old.

Mpintimpi, being a tiny village, could not boast enough children to justify the setting up of a primary school—we had to walk to Nyafoman, a bigger settlement three kilometres north of our own.

Despite the hassle of walking to school, I loved going to school.

When I got to Primary 5, something happened to me to threaten an abrupt end of my educational carrier. All of a sudden, and for no apparent cause, my left ankle began to swell up. Initially, the accompanying discomfort was bearable, permitting me to continue to attend school. In time, however, the pain increased in intensity to the point that I could no longer walk to school. It led to a two-year interruption in my education.

By the hands of Providence, and contrary to all my expectations, I managed to resume my education. Not only that, the village boy that I was ended up attending Mfantsipim School, one of the leading secondary schools in the country.

In June 1978, I sat for the General Certificate of Education Advanced Level, more commonly known as the GCE A-Level examination. I was desirous of studying medicine. I yearned not only to understand the cause of the condition of my left ankle but also to contribute to improving the healthcare conditions of my community in particular and Ghana in general.

I put in extra effort in my preparations for the exams to ensure I obtained the grades that would guarantee me a place in medical school.

Thus far, I have provided a brief account of my beginning to the time of completing my sixth form. I will discuss further details of my life's journey during my narration.

My conversion story

Having provided a short background of myself, I now turn to the story of how I became a Christian.

Before I continue my conversion story, I want to point out one fact: in the society where I grew up, and I dare say it holds for the whole of Ghana and perhaps Africa in general, hardly anyone questions the existence of Almighty God.

Restricting myself to the Akan ethnic group of Ghana to which I belong, our ancestors always believed in *Twediampong Nyakopon.*

For those not at home in the Twi language, *Tweadeapong* means Almighty, *Nyankopong* on its part, means God. Yes, the Akans consider *Tweadeapong Nyankopong*, Almighty God in English, as being the Creator of the Universe.

From the preceding, it becomes clear that neither European missionaries nor Islamic conquerors introduced the belief in Almighty God into our culture. Indeed, from time immemorial, our ancestors believed in *Twediampon Nyankopon* (Almighty God*)*, who dwells far beyond the skies.

The main difference between the manner the ancestors worshipped only one God and the Way Christians do lies in the intermediary between humanity and the Almighty God.

Whereas Christianity points to the Lord Jesus Christ as the only way one can reach God, our ancestors and present-day adherents of several traditional African religions, on their part, believe that they can do so utilizing mediums such as rivers, stones, mountains, animals, etc.

When I was growing up in my little village, there were two churches in the settlement—the Presbyterian and the Christ Apostolic churches. That number has, in the meantime, increased to five.

My parents did not consider themselves Christians. Instead, they were adherents of a traditional form of worship. Later in life, Papa, through a dramatic encounter, became a Christian and set up his church.

Mother, on her part, did not join any church during her lifetime.

Her main reason for not joining a church was not because she did not believe in God. Instead, she stayed away from church because of what she called her "disappointment in the lifestyles of the churchgoers".

"You of this generation are not living according to your Christian calling; you are instead taking undue advantage of God's longsuffering nature towards His children," she lamented. Once a year, the church held harvest and thanksgiving services to raise funds—that was when Mother attended and contributed financially to the running of the church.

Though my parents stayed away from the church, they did not prevent their children from doing so. Together with my other siblings, we attended the Presbyterian church quite regularly.

I attended the Roman Catholic Primary school. It was a state school. Though a state school, we began the day with a short Christian meditation.

I moved to Oda Secondary School, a boarding school in the district capital. You may ask: how did the child of impoverished peasant farmers manage to attend a boarding school? The brief answer is that initially, Ranford, my senior brother, supported me. Later, I was granted a government scholarship.

Though a state school, the morning assemblies before the beginning of lessons were Christian based; the same thing could be said of the weekly Sunday evening worship services.

Others may wonder why a secular school held Christian-based morning assemblies and Sunday worship services. I shall provide a short explanation. There are three main religions in Ghana: Christianity, Islam and traditional African worship.

Adherents of the Islamic faith, about 10% of the population, are mainly in the north of the country. The rest of the country is predominantly Christian, with small minority adherents of various traditional African forms of worship.

My Alma Mater, Oda Secondary School, is in the Eastern Region, a mainly Christian area. Indeed, only a handful of people of the Islamic faith attended our school.

Despite my belief in God, and also enjoying the Christian worship services at school, I was not a committed Christian. Indeed, I only occasionally read the Bible. During the holidays when I didn't have to attend church, I rarely did so.

The best way to describe me in matters of faith at that time was a person who accepted God's presence but was not committed to fellowshipping with Him.

Yes, the universal suffering in the presence of a loving God seriously challenged my faith. Whenever something terrible happened to me personally and the world at large, the question that came to mind was: if there was a loving God, why should the world be full of so much evil?—war, crime, injustice, confusion here, confusion there, confusion everywhere!

My difficulty with serving God who allowed suffering in the world, changed on the 14th September 1978.

On that day, a good acquaintance of mine visited me. During our conversation, she narrated her touching conversion story, which eventually influenced my decision to accept the Lord into my life.

Before I detail the said meeting, allow me to briefly narrate an experience I had a few weeks before the encounter, which would highly influence my decision on that fateful day.

As mentioned earlier, I moved from my little village of Mpintimpi to attend Oda Secondary School. In 1976, I sat for my General Certificate of Education Ordinary Levels (GCE "O" Levels) at Oda Secondary School. From there, I moved to Mfantsipim School in Cape Coast to do my two-year sixth-form course.

One Sunday, towards the end of my second and final year at Mfantsipim School, rumours began to circulate to the effect that one of the students in the junior classes had gone missing. As it later turned out, he had died in a road traffic accident the previous day as he was returning from a visit to his friend in a nearby girls boarding school. The vehicle he was hitch-hiking in on the approximately 25-kilometres drive back to school crashed about midway through the journey, killing the two occupants instantly.

Although I knew him only casually, his tragic death at the age of about 15 years sent shock waves through me. All of a sudden the awareness that life could end very suddenly came home to me pretty powerfully and gave me food for thought. Before the body of our companion was driven to his hometown for burial, a memorial service was held in the large school chapel in his honour. At one stage in the solemn service we were permitted to file past the body to pay our last respects to the dead.

Up to that time I had witnessed a couple of funeral ceremonies at Mpintimpi.

As the dead lay in state, various mourners drew near to pay their respect. Children were generally not permitted to go too close. For the first time, however, I was experiencing a close confrontation with the dead. Our mate, who a couple of days before was going about his life like any young person of his age, now lay motionless before us. Where, I wondered, would he spend his eternity?

Mfantsipim School boasts of being the oldest secondary school in Ghana. It was founded in 1876 by Methodist missionaries to the then Gold Coast. Though it had since been taken over by the state, it still adhered to the Methodist tradition. In morning assemblies and Sunday evening worship we sang from the Methodist hymn book; that was also the case at the funeral service of our late schoolmate. Among the songs we sang on the solemn occasion was hymn 157:

> Jesus Calls us! Over the tumult
>   of our life's wild restless sea,
>   Day by day His sweet voice
>   soundeth
> Saying: Christian follow me.
>
>   As of old, apostles heard it
>   By the Galilean lake,
>   Turned from home and toil and kindren
>   Leaving all for His dear sake.
>
>   Jesus calls us from the worship
>   Of the vain world's golden store,
>   From each idol that would keep us,
>   Saying: Christian love Me more!
>
>   In our joys and in our sorrows,
>   Days of toil and hours of ease,
>   Still He calls, in cares and pleasures,
>   That we love Him more than
>   these.
>
>   Jesus calls us! By thy mercies,
>   Saviour, make us hear Thy call
>   Give our hearts to Thine obedience.
>   Serve and Love Thee best of all.

I am not a person easily overtaken by emotion. As we went through that song, however, the words touched my heart to the extent that I could hardly suppress my tears. I began to reflect on the hymn.

As already mentioned, though I believed in God, one could at best describe me as a nominal Christian, not committed in my faith. Yet on that day, as we were bidding goodbye to our departed classmate, the new call of Jesus our Lord seemed to come personally to me—to follow Him; the call came home even more powerfully to me. Even as we sang the song I dipped my hand into my pocket, removed a pen and placed a big mark on the hymn number: 157. That was the only song in the whole book to be singled out that way.

Over the next several days the death of my schoolmate occupied my mind. The thought that I could face a similar fate at any time would not leave me in peace. Should something like that happen to me, where would I spend eternity?

Soon life returned to normal. I continued to attend Sunday evening worship service, as was required of every student, without any conscious commitment to leave this 'world's vain golden store' to follow Jesus, as the hymn invited me to do.

The two-year sixth-form course at Mfantsipim ended in June 1978. In anticipation of the results and my admission to medical school the following October, I bade farewell to my Alma Mater and headed for Mpintimpi.

After spending a few days there, I headed for Accra. My goal was to find a vacation job to keep me occupied and earn money ahead of my admission to medical school.

I lived in a suburb of the city known as Asylum Down. I lived in the same apartment building as my brother Ransford and his family. Because their small flat barely had enough space for himself and his family, I stayed with some friends who happened to have rented an apartment just adjacent to Ransford's.

One day I went on a stroll through the streets in our neighbourhood. While roaming about, I unexpectedly bumped into an old acquaintance, Grace, the cousin of George, who was my best friend at Oda Secondary school. As it turned out, she resided in an apartment block not far from ours.

A few days after our chance meeting, she visited me at home. During the visit, she spoke enthusiastically about her new-found joy in Christ and invited me also to accept the Lord. "God so loved the world that He sent His only begotten son, that whoever believes in Him will not perish but have eternal life."' She smiled and looked at me expectantly.

I looked in bewilderment at her. Though I did not know her closely, from the reports I had heard about her, she would be the last person one would expect to be talking about faith in Christ!

She earnestly implored me to accept the Lord. "If the Lord sets you free, you will be free indeed," she added.

She asked me to think over our conversation. She would be delighted to see me in her church. She could call on me the following Sunday to take me to her church if I so wished.

After interacting for about an hour, she begged to leave. I then escorted her to the gate.

As I pondered over the conversation with Grace on my return to our flat, my eyes caught sight of my Methodist Hymn Book from Mfantsipim School. It happened to be lying in one corner of the writing desk.

Even to this day, I cannot explain why I decided to pick it up. The moment I got hold of it, behold, it opened at Hymn 157, the only hymn marked in the book, the very hymn that had spoken to my heart so powerfully a few months before at the funeral in Mfantsipim. The words of the song stared me in the face. I read through the whole hymn, verse by verse. I re-read it the second time. Goose pimples formed all over my body as I went through the lines. For a while, I could hardly control my tears.

Grace's testimony alone might not have moved my stony heart. That sign—the hymn book opening spontaneously at the page with the hymn with the first line, "Jesus calls us over the tumult of our life's wild, restless sea"—following closely on her testimony, served as the proverbial last straw needed to break the back of the camel.

"The Lord has found you at last," a still voice within me seemed to say. "In the past, you did not heed the call. This time there is nowhere you can run to." An unusual quiet filled the room. Without knowing what I was doing, I was on my knees, praying. When I got up, I looked out for a Bible. There were a couple of them in the room. I got hold of one and began reading it. Suddenly, the words began to speak to my heart in a manner I had not experienced before.

I followed the invitation of my good acquaintance and attended her church the following Sunday, September 17, 1978. Pastor Ofosu-Mensah, the pastor of the Open Bible Church, as the church is known, delivered a touching sermon on my first visit.

As was his custom, at the end of his sermon, he asked those wishing to give their lives to the Lord to come to the altar to be prayed for. Without hesitation, I heeded the call. Another worshipper joined me. After congratulating us on our decision, he asked the whole church to rise as he prayed for us. Amid the cheerful applause and shouts of "Welcome home! Welcome home!" we returned to our seats.

* * *

Thus far, I have provided a brief account of the circumstances of my conversion. I was not baptized as a child. Burning with enthusiasm, I grasped the first opportunity that availed itself. It came on December 23, 1978.

Together with other members of my church, I underwent water baptism at the Labadi beach in Accra. For those unfamiliar with the term 'water baptism': in contrast to the baptism conducted through the sprinkling of water on the head of the one undergoing it, water baptism involves the complete immersion of the body in water.

I actively practised my faith throughout my time in Ghana. Bubbling with energy, enthusiasm and fire, I rarely missed any church activity.

Besides the regular Sunday morning worship service, we also had Sunday evening service. Wednesday evening was time for Bible study. Friday was set aside as a day of fasting and prayer. Except on medical grounds, our pastor encouraged members to partake in the fast. We stayed away from food and fluids from waking up in the morning till around 6 pm.

Adventure to Europe

As I have just recently mentioned, when I was awaiting my A-Level results I made a conscious decision to follow the Lord, yes, when I underwent what Christians refer to as a 'born-again' experience.

When I was sitting for my GCE A-Level and just a nominal believer in God, my wish was to gain admission to medical school. You might ask: How could someone from a poor home pay his way through medical school?

The answer is that though it was financially challenging for students from a poor background to go to university, it was not beyond possible due to the generous government funding scheme in place at that time.

Firstly, tuition was free from primary school up to university in the country.

Secondly, the state provided university students free accommodation and three free meals daily.

As if that were not enough: students could also apply for a loan to pay for textbooks and other educational materials.

The only challenge I faced was acquiring one of the few medical school places on offer.

As I write this report in the middle of 2022, there are seven medical schools in Ghana; five are public, and two are private.

At the time in question, there were only two universities with faculties for medicine. Between them, the two universities admitted around eighty students annually. As might be expected, the competition was tough.

Conscious that only top grades could land me one of the highly contested vacancies, I prepared well for my exams.

Not long after my conversion experience, the A-Level results were released.

I was disappointed with my results, aware I could have done better than I did. Nevertheless, my grades fulfilled the admission requirements of both medical schools. Indeed, a mate of mine, whose grades were just about my own, gained entrance. He boasted something I could only dream of, though—parents of influence, yes, well-connected parents.

Without such interconnection to people of influence I missed the chance of gaining admission to medical school. The selection board didn't even consider it necessary to invite me for an interview. Instead, they offered me the chance to do a bachelor's degree in the sciences—a field of study that was far from my favourite.

As expected, I was very disheartened by the turn of events.

As I struggled to come to terms with the setback, a friend directed my attention to the Eastern Bloc Scholarship scheme. Under this scheme, countries of the then-Eastern Bloc countries offered scholarships to students of the developing world to study in their various countries.

After submitting an application, I was invited to attend an interview. A few days later I received the good news—my application was successful.

Just as I was rejoicing with the prospect of studying medicine in the Soviet Union, one day I woke up to the shocking news that my name had been dropped from the list!

Thus I missed my second opportunity of studying medicine. Just as my world seemed to crumble around me, I saw a ray of light pointing to the then-West Germany. Why West Germany, one might ask? Two main factors accounted for my newfound hope.

In the first place, I learnt that tuition was free in German universities for every student, foreigners alike.

Secondly, the cousin of my good friend George who I referred to earlier, yes, the lady whose testimony led me to my conversion, had just moved to Germany with her husband. She promised to do what she could to assist me in the initial stages of my stay in Germany, should I manage to make it there.

With that background information, I sat down to consider how I could make my way to West Germany.

I established that there were two avenues at my disposal. I might refer to them as the 'official' and 'unofficial' routes.

The official pathway was to pay for a German language class in Accra. After passing a test in basic German, I could apply to various German universities. If I got one of them to offer me admission, I would approach the German Embassy to apply for a student visa.

But this was not plausible, given that my parents could not afford to assist me financially.

Next was the unofficial pathway. This involved me acquiring a round ticket from Accra to East Berlin. With that ticket, I would approach the embassy of East Germany in Accra to apply for a transit visa for East Berlin. Once in East Berlin, I could move to West Berlin. Once in West Berlin, part of West Germany, I could apply to the university of my choice.

Even though the hurdles presented by the unofficial pathway seemed less arduous, it was still a non-starter for me, for I did not have the means to acquire the round ticket flight from Accra to East Berlin.

Notwithstanding the seemingly impossible hurdles, I was still determined to pursue my path to medical school.

Just about that time I met a friend who told me he was on his way to Lagos to work for his ticket to enable him to travel to the US to fulfil his dream of studying architecture.

At that time, Nigeria was a great attraction for Ghanaians and nationals from the whole of the West African region.

The oil-rich nation's economy had received a big boost resulting from the sharp rise in the price of crude oil following the oil crisis of 1979.

The country needed several hands to work on the countless building and construction projects throughout the large country. The buoyant economy had also led the federal government to introduce free education for all. Several new schools had been established to cope with the increased number of pupils enrolling. The huge demand for teachers that had arisen due to that policy could not be satisfied by local staff alone. As former English colonies, Ghana and Nigeria had a similar educational structure. Teachers from Ghana were thus highly welcomed in Nigeria. News soon spread to Ghana in this regard. Several

Ghanaians left to take up appointments in the comparatively wealthy Nigeria.

Thanks to a friend of mine who arranged a loan from his sister, I left Ghana on Monday, December 1, 1980, in the company of my friend Gyasi.

On my arrival in Nigeria, I initially worked on construction sites for a while before gaining employment as a teacher in a secondary school.

The opportunity to attempt my journey to Europe presented itself a little over eighteen months after being in my teaching position—namely, when I managed to save the amount needed for my adventure to Europe.

At the beginning of May 1982, I purchased a plane ticket—a return trip from Lagos to East Berlin and back. Armed with this ticket, I visited the embassy of the then-German Democratic Republic in Lagos and applied for a transit visa for East Berlin.

Armed with the transit visa for East Berlin, I left Lagos on May 11, 1982, on a Balkan Airlines flight and headed for Europe. On my arrival in East Berlin, I finally made it to West Berlin.

After surmounting several seemingly insurmountable challenges, I enrolled at the Hanover medical school in October 1984.

After training as a GP, I worked in Germany for a while before moving to the UK in 2006.

Disappointed Expectations

So far, I have provided the reader with the background information about myself, my pre-university education in Ghana, my conversion story and how I made it to Europe.

I now turn to the question: what was my expectation of the state of European Christianity before setting foot on the continent?

The answer to that question is that I thought Christianity was well established on "the old continent", as writers and historians affectionately refer to Europe.

Indeed, my expectation was that in the same way churches in my native Ghana were filled with worshipers on Sundays, that would also be the case in Germany and Western Europe in general.

Concerning Eastern Europe, I was aware the communists suppressed the church, forcing it to go underground. You may ask: how did you know this when you had not been there? The answer is that I had contact with some of my schoolmates who were beneficiaries of the Eastern Scholarships, scholarships placed at the disposal of developing countries by the Eastern Bloc of countries to enable students from such countries to study in the Soviet bloc. They came back with reports that the churches there had been forced underground. Occasionally during service, our pastor asked us to join him in prayers for Christians suffering persecution worldwide, including those in the communist countries of Eastern Europe and elsewhere in the world.

Though, as already indicated, I had no clear idea of the state of the church in Western Europe, I presumed that Christianity was well established in that part of the world and that church services would be well attended on Sundays.

Several factors influenced my thought concerning Christianity in Europe.

The first school I attended in my academic journey was Nyafoman Roman Catholic Primary school. It is a state school run by the Catholic Church,

Though it admits pupils irrespective of their religious affiliation, by virtue of its connection to the Catholic church, the pastor in charge of the dioceses visits the school occasionally.

At that time, our "Roman Father", as we called our pastor, was of European descent.

During such visits, the whole school gathered in the assembly hall for a short Catholic mass. That led my young mind to think that all people of European descent were Christians.

Later in my academic journey, I learnt that European missionaries, like David Livingstone, introduced Christianity to Africa.

Still later in life, I read about the works of influential European Christians, the likes of John Wesley, Martin Luther, John Calvin, etc.

Furthermore, during my elementary school days, it was a trend among me and some of my peers to write to missionary societies in the USA and Europe to request Christian literature—Bibles, New Testaments, pamphlets, etc. The fact that the organizations we wrote to generously responded to our requests led my young mind to presume residents of their countries were devoted Christians keen on sharing the Gospel.

The Open Bible Church occasionally hosted guest preachers from Europe and the US. As I write, the inspiring sermons preached by some of our visiting European and American evangelists are still fresh in memory.

Still, dwelling on the factors which led me to think Europeans held firmly to the Christian faith: in those days, the televangelists Oral Roberts and Billy Graham were household names in Ghana. I, in particular, went to great lengths to ensure I did not miss Oral Roberts's weekly Sunday evening appearance on Ghana Broadcasting Corporation TV (GBC-TV), the state TV channel.

The reader might want to ask why the two American-based preachers led me to think Christianity played an important role in the life of Europeans. The reader may pardon me because I was young and naive, leading me to draw that illogical conclusion.

* * *

It would not take very long after I arrived in Europe, for it to dawn on me that the state of Christianity in Europe was far from what I had envisaged. The realization was not immediate, however. Indeed, initially I had a pleasant church experience in my new home, which led me to think my expectations of the state of Christianity in Europe had been met.

As expected, on my arrival in West Berlin, I was desirous of finding a church in which to worship. The opportunity came my way a few days after my arrival.

Whilst on a visit to the city centre, my attention was drawn to a tall Victorian-style church building that was partly destroyed at the top. A few metres next to the old building was a modern one. The cross it bore on its roof revealed its use.

Later I got to know some historical facts about the partly destroyed church.

Construction work on the building began in 1891 and ended in 1895. It was partly destroyed during a bombing raid on Berlin in 1943.

After the war, the authorities planned to replace it. This met with the protest of the population, which led the authorities to change their mind. Eventually, a new church was built beside the old one, the old one being kept as a memorial to the destructive forces of war. The old building has become a tourist attraction. Like many of those roaming that area of Berlin on that beautiful day in spring, I entered the old building to view it from within.

Whilst on my rounds through the church, I came across a leaflet placed there by the Lutheran American Church in Berlin which, as I found out later, served the civilian population connected with the American military stationed there at the time.

I made contact with Gary, the pastor, who directed me to the church. When I visited them the following Sunday, I was pleasantly surprised. The attendance was good, the service was lively, and the worshippers were very friendly and welcoming.

If I thought this positive experience reflected the general situation of the church in West Berlin and Europe at large, I would be disappointed.

Later, when I attended typical German Lutheran churches, I realized the churches were sparsely attended—mainly by the elderly.

Where, I wondered, were the youth and young adults, yes, the future generation?

In time it dawned on me that Christianity today hardly played a role in the population's life, especially the youth. They made merry on Saturdays and slept through the Sunday mornings.

Indeed, on Sunday mornings the roads were virtually deserted; if one came across anyone heading for church, that individual would likely be middle-aged or older.

I have, in the meantime, spent over 40 years in Europe. If the state of Christianity in Europe in the 1980s filled me with sorrow, 40 years living in the situation is wrenching my heart!

What, then, has led to the present state of affairs? Why has Europe deserted the 'glad tidings', the good news of salvation preached by Jesus?

PART 2
A brief look at the history of European Christianity

The advent of Christianity to Europe

Before I set about to consider what in my view has led to the dire situation of European Christianity, I want to take the reader through a brief history of Christianity—from the first time it arrived on the European continent to the present day. As already indicated, I will provide only a brief overview. Those looking for a more detailed account may contact the relevant literature.

From the accounts of the Gospel and historians, the Lord Jesus Christ began his public ministry aged around 30 years. Three years later he was arrested, tried by what can aptly be described as a kangaroo court, sentenced to death by crucifixion, and the sentence hurriedly executed.

Just as he had predicted during his lifetime, he was resurrected on the third day. Thereafter he revealed himself to his followers on several occasions. Forty days after the historic event he ascended into heaven before the gathering of a sizable number of his followers.

He promised the coming of the Holy Spirit, which duly happened on a day that became known as the Day of Pentecost.

Imbued with the power of the Holy Spirit, his disciples spread the Gospel. Thus, starting from Jerusalem, the Gospel, the good news of the Kingdom of God, was broadcast abroad. The biblical book of Acts records the rapid spread of the Gospel from Jerusalem to Rome through Samaria, Antioch, Asia, and Europe.

Concerning the arrival of Christianity to Europe, the first recorded individual to have accepted the Gospel was a resident of the Greek city, Philippi, by the name of Lydia. The New Testament book of Acts Chapter 16: 14-15 provides an account of her conversion:

> *And a certain woman named Lydia, a seller of purple, of the city of Thyatira, which worshipped God, heard us: whose heart the Lord opened, that she attended unto the things which were spoken of Paul.*
>
> *And when she was baptized, and her household, she besought us, saying, If ye have judged me to be faithful to the Lord, come into my house, and abide there. And she constrained us.* Acts 16:14-15 KJV

The spread of the Gospel into the Roman Empire was not without opposition. Indeed, adherents of the new faith would soon be subjected to persecution. Following a devastating fire in Rome in AD 64, Emperor Nero singled out the Christians and the Jewish community for blame. Many Christians were arrested and put to death—in the main through burning.

An epic moment in the spread of Christianity in the Roman Empire came on October 28, 321 AD. The forces of Emperor Constantine prevailed over those of his rival, Emperor Maxentius, in the Battle of the Milvian Bridge that took place that day. His victory over Maxentius made Constantine the sole Emperor of the Roman Empire.

Emperor Constantine bore testimony to seeing a cross in the skies a night before the battle with the inscription: "By this will you win your victory." He thus attributed his victory to the intervention of the Christian God. That experience led to his Christian conversion.

Thus from 321 AD onwards, Christianity became the Emperor's religion, and a few years later, it became the official religion of the Roman Empire.

In the 4th century, Emperor Theodosius, through the Edict of Thessalonica, made Christianity (notably Catholicism) the Roman Empire's official religion.

Christianity spread throughout the Roman Empire. By the time Rome fell in 476, much of Europe was Christian.

Reformation

Christianity, specifically Catholicism, dominated the lives of European peasants and nobility during the Middle Ages (500-1500 AD). Religious institutions, including the Church and the monasteries, were wealthy and influential.

Corruption of the church in the Middle Ages led Martin Luther to publish the *Ninety-five Theses*, challenging papal authority and criticizing its perceived corruption, particularly concerning the sale of indulgences.

Luther pinned his Ninety-five Theses aimed at the reformation of the Catholic church to the walls of his church at Wittenberg in Germany on October 31, 1517. That deed sparked the Reformation movement, which would see the split of the Church into Catholic and Protestant. It is beyond the realm of this book to go into further detail on the matter.

Impact of Christianity on Europe

Christianity, without a doubt, has massively impacted European society.

This is evidenced by the numerous cathedrals that, to this day, adorn many European towns and cities.

Christianity helped to liberate Europe from paganism, superstition and ignorance, while the monasteries are credited with having laid the foundation for establishing institutions of higher learning, such as universities in the Roman Empire. Indeed, Christianity played an essential role in the formation of institutions of modern education in Europe and, for that matter, the rest of the world.

One can say that the church created the basis of the Western educational system. The Medieval Church not only founded but also funded a good proportion of the institutions of higher learning during the Middle Ages. Such institutions played leading roles in research in medicine, science and technology.

The church's impact was felt not only in education, health, economics, and politics but also in social affairs, e.g., marriage and family.

European missionary activities

Before I leave this subject, I want to mention the vital role European missionaries played in the spread of Christianity around the world. In this connection, special mention should be made of the period between 1500 and 1750. That period indeed brought a dramatic change in missionary activities, resulting in the spread of Christianity around the world.

Two main reasons account for the development.

Firstly, Luther's reformation unleashed missionary fervour, not only among the Protestants but also among Catholics, with the two groups competing for converts.

The second reason for the spread of Christianity was the Age of Exploration. By the 1500s Europeans travelled the seas to almost every part of the globe. Missionaries followed the European conquerors, traders, and colonists.

PART 3A

The decline of European Christianity

Intro

Thus far, I have given a brief account of the church's history in Europe and the vital role European missionaries played in the spread of Christianity around the world.

Having provided a brief run through the history of Christianity in Europe, I want to dwell on the decline of the church in Europe. Why then have a good many Europeans turned their backs on the Gospel?

Before I start, I want to make one thing clear from the outset. This is not an academic dissertation. No, I am not presenting a scholastic treatise, a scholarly thesis carefully compiled after thorough research employing the standard tools and pathways of educational research—accessing and evaluating various forms of information, then carefully scrutinizing the data obtained before coming to a conclusion on the state of Christianity in Europe.

In other words, I did not, for example, send out questionnaires to, say, a hundred thousand individuals spread across Europe to ask about their views on Christianity, their attitude to the church, whether they believed in God and then drawing conclusions based on their responses.

No, that, dear reader, is not what I have undertaken.

Instead, what you are about to read is based on the insights gained over the 40 years I have lived almost uninterruptedly in Europe. I did not live in isolation from the European population. Taking Germany as an example, right from the beginning of my arrival there, I interacted closely with the German people, in the church, at the University, and in hospitals where I worked.

Later, as a family doctor (GP), I visited the homes of patients who, for various reasons, could not attend the doctor's practice/ surgery themselves. Through visiting them as a doctor and not as an evangelist, I gained in time a fair idea of their thinking about the Christian faith.

* * *

I don't want others to refer to me as a moral apostle. Furthermore, I do not want to create the impression of possessing absolute truths on religious matters. I have not seen God. I have not spoken to Him face-to-face; that, however, does not mean I do not know Him, or see His presence.

Do we, after all, see radio waves to feel their effects on what we do?

I am not forcing anyone to side with me.

I am open to debate, but politely.

I do not want anyone to brand me as radical, conservative, or dangerous. I am just speaking my mind in a democratic society. You may accept it or leave it.

The factors I am about to touch upon are not unique to Europe; they could also be true in other parts of the world, especially the rest of the Western World. This discourse, however, is about Europe, Western Europe in particular, so I will limit my arguments and examples to Europe.

* * *

I have chosen to adopt a two-tier approach in my presentation of the state of Christianity in Europe. First, I will touch on the factors briefly. I am doing so with deliberate intention. It will permit readers who may not have the time to spare to get the gist of the matter and move on. For those wishing for a more detailed discussion of the issues, I will return to each of the factors to discuss them in detail.

I mentioned earlier that on my arrival in Europe in May, 1982, I was disappointed with the state of Christianity in Europe.

If you ask me how I feel about the state of the Gospel of Christ in Europe during November 2022, my answer is that I was, and still am, heartbroken, yes deeply saddened. Indeed, all statistics point to a persistently declining number of worshippers over the last several years. I am not a prophet to foresee the future, but should the current trend continue, it is anyone's guess how European Christianity will fare 50 years from now.

The question that comes to mind is:

Why has a good proportion—if not the majority—of present-day Europeans rejected (or at best become indifferent to) the Christian message of salvation, the good news of the Cross, which offers stability in an unstable world and gives strength to the soul?

Why are the churches empty on Sundays when on the other hand, the football stadia, pop concerts and other entertainment venues are overbooked?

Why do Europeans flock to the beaches, football stadia, and other Sunday events and leave the churches empty?

Of course, I have nothing against others enjoying their pastimes in good and bad weather. I would have wished, however, that they devoted at least a wee bit of their time to advance the faith of their ancestors.

Often I ask myself the question: What does a good proportion of the European population find offensive with the soothing and reassuring words of the Lord Jesus Christ, the liberating words of the Gospel, such as the following?

Come unto me, all ye that labour and are heavy laden, and I will give you rest.

Take my yoke upon you, and learn of me; for I am meek and lowly in heart: and ye shall find rest unto your souls. Matthew 11:28-29

I am the good shepherd: the good shepherd giveth his life for the sheep. But he that is an hireling, and not the shepherd, whose own the sheep are not, seeth the wolf coming, and leaveth the sheep, and fleeth: and the wolf catcheth them, and scattereth the sheep. The hireling fleeth, because he is an hireling, and careth not for the sheep. I am the good shepherd, and know my sheep, and am known of mine. As the Father knoweth me, even so know I the Father: and I lay down my life for the sheep. John 10:11-15

So if the Son sets you free, you will be free indeed. John 8:36

Empty promises, someone would tell me to the face.

To that, I will reply: How can you have an opinion of something you have not tried yourself? You have got to try it for yourself; yes, you have to taste it to enjoy the sweetness of the Gospel.

PART 3B

Brief overview of the factors leading to the decline of European Christianity

Based on the insights I have gained during my forty-year stay in Europe—insights gained through direct conversation with friends, colleagues, and acquaintances, as well as reading from and viewing the popular press and reading literature on the matter—I will humbly present the factors below as having contributed and continue to contribute to the decline of Christianity on the continent.

I want to stress at the outset that I do not claim authority in anything; the reader is free to accept or reject my viewpoints and postulations.

In this chapter, I will touch briefly on the factors; in the subsequent chapters, I will touch upon them in some detail.

A) Science & Technology

Insights gained through scientific research and technological advancement have led some to question the existence of Almighty God. I want to break down this theme into three categories:

i) The Big Bang Theory

The Big Bang Theory holds that the universe as we know it started with an infinitely hot and dense single point that expanded and stretched—first at unimaginable speeds and then at a more measurable rate—to form the universe as we know it today. According to the theory, the so-called 'big bang' happened around 13.8 billion years ago.

The bottom line of the theory is that the universe came about by an accidental event that happened several billion years ago. In other words, the theory has no room for a creator God who called everything into being.

Though a theory, many world residents, especially in Europe and the rest of the Western World, consider it credible.

ii) The Theory of Evolution by natural selection as postulated by Charles Darwin.

It is beyond the remit of this book to delve into the details and intricacies of Darwin's theory of evolution. The theory postulates that all organisms have their source in a primordial cell. The theory of evolution is incompatible with the Creation Story as thought by scripture—more of that later.

iii) Fossil finds by palaeontologists

From time to time, we read headlines concerning fossil finds made here and there. Accompanying the so-called 'breaking news' are wild conjectures by the so-called experts concerning the ages of the fossils and the age of the universe in general.

Such wild speculations and conjectures concerning the alleged age of the universe provide needed ammunition to those who question the authenticity of the Bible and the existence of a Creator God.

B) Perceived contradictions in the Bible

A good deal of Europeans I have interacted with point to perceived contradictions in the Bible to question its reliability and authenticity.

In my interaction with Europeans, I realize some have difficulty with the Bible. Many indeed struggle with sections of the Old Testament. I still remember someone I tried to evangelize in Germany, accusing God of permitting the Israelites to commit genocide against other nations. I will return to the matter at a later stage.

C) Perceived failings of the established churches past and present

In my interactions with individuals who have turned their backs on the church, some are quick to cite the shortcomings of various churches, in particular, the established ones—Catholic, Lutheran, Anglican etc. as contributing towards turning their backs on Christianity.

On not a few occasions, when I tried to evangelize individuals in Germany, they cited the support some in the clergy offered Hitler for their rejection of what the church stands for.

In recent times, headlines reporting the involvement of a section of the clergy in child sexual abuse has damaged the reputation of the church even further.

D) The politicization of the church

Some are shunning the church because, in their opinion, it has become politicized. Indeed, in several European countries, the established churches draw financial support from the state. Much as it gives it financial security, it constrains the hands of the church in its core mission to preach the Gospel of salvation.

The word of God does not change; societal trends do.

The saying has it that 'He who pays the piper calls the tune'.

Therein lies the conflict. The church has to preach the word of God without fear or favour. A church depending on the state for support, may not have the nerve to challenge the state should it pass legislation that contradicts Biblical principles. Furthermore, owing to the fact that a government is supporting the church, the church may tend to take a stance on a political issue and thus alienate a section of the population with a different view on the political issue.

E) Confusion concerning which religion holds the truth

Observing European society first-hand, I have realized there exists a great deal of confusion about religion, especially among the younger generation.

As I mentioned earlier, in several societies, including the one prevailing in my native Ghana, there is a general belief in the supernatural. The situation is different in Europe. A sizeable proportion of European children grow up in homes where adults believe in nothing. Even if they believe in God and are Christians, they may classify themselves as non-practicing. Under such circumstances, they are unlikely to pass on their faith to their children.

Such children are likely to fill their religious void with various kinds of ideas, philosophies and ideologies. The result is that individuals grow up in European societies confused about belief in the supernatural, to put it mildly

F) The European mindset

One of the obstacles in the acceptance of Christianity in Europe derives from the European tendency to only accept facts after rigorous debate. It operates on the premise that truth can only be derived through logical, rigorous arguments. Whatever is not logical or rational is rejected. The European mindset seems to be based on the premise of "seeing is believing".

Generally, the European / Western mindset derived from the period of Enlightenment, the intellectual and philosophical movement that dominated Europe in the 17th and 18th centuries. The Enlightenment included a range of ideas centred on the value of human happiness, the pursuit of knowledge obtained through employing reason and the evidence of the senses and ideals such as liberty, progress, tolerance, fraternity, constitutional government, and separation of church and state.

That mode of thinking and reasoning is helpful in world affairs; it cannot be replicated in humankind's relationship with Almighty God, the Big Boss of Creation, as I tend to call him. I will deal with the matter in some detail later.

G) Catastrophes, sufferings, injustices etc. in the face of a loving God

Where was God on September 11, 2001, when the militant Islamic extremist network al-Qaeda carried out four coordinated suicide terrorist attacks against the United States, killing thousands and injuring tens of thousands?

Where was God during the terror attack in Paris on Friday, November 13, 2017, which left 130 people dead and hundreds wounded?

Why did God allow the COVID-19 outbreak?

Why didn't Almighty God prevent wars like World War I & II?

Where is God in the Russian-Ukraine war?

Why doesn't God speak sense into the minds of those causing mayhem all over the globe?

The list of the 'Why not's?' directed at the Almighty by humankind is unending.

Personal suffering and general misery in the presence of an Almighty God have challenged and continue to challenge the faith of others. It challenges, in particular, the European mindset, which, as already pointed out, is grounded on logic and rational thinking.

More of that later.

H) Wars past and present

In my interactions with my European friends on matters related to my faith, some cited the devastation brought on Europe and the rest of the world by World War I & II for their negative attitude towards God. "Well, He may exist," one of my German friends told me, "I cannot, however, worships such a God; I am sorry!"

Even as I write these lines in June 2022, the deaths, human suffering, material destruction, financial losses, etc., brought about by the war in Ukraine raises questions in the minds of many concerning God's existence.

I) Poverty among populations who hold on to Christianity

In my conversation over the years with my European friends, work colleagues, acquaintances, etc., I have, on many occasions, been confronted with statements like the following:

> "Friend, you in Africa go to church every Sunday. You call yourselves religious. Despite devoutly worshipping God, your continent is in a miserable state. Why do you recommend Him to me if your God is not helping you out of your misery?"

J) Difficulty coming to terms with the concept of Satan, demons, principalities

My impression from living in Europe over 40 years is that many of the population hold an attitude that can be expressed in the words "seeing is believing". What is not seen, or validated by scientific research, is not believed. Following on such lines, many Europeans not only reject the existence of God, but also the reality of Satan, demons, witchcraft, principalities, etc.

K) Humanistic worldview

Put briefly, humanism is the idea that the human being is the centre of everything and that there is no Divine power for one to be subject to. Life is our own, so we can do whatever we wish with our lives. To bring the message of salvation through Christ to individuals holding such a view is daunting, to put it mildly. My interactions with the population have led me to conclude that a good proportion of the European population entertain such a view.

L) Prosperity and the European Welfare State system

Western Europe has grown wealthy over the years. Not only have the individuals become prosperous, but the nations on the continent have grown generally wealthy. Prosperity has permitted various countries to introduce a generous welfare state system that cares for those who fall through the social net. With their material needs taken care of by their respective governments, many do not see the need to look up to an invisible power to provide for them.

M) Social Media

Long before the advent of the internet, the church in Europe was already in decline. Social media culture has only tended to aggravate an already bad situation. I will return to the matter later.

N) Miscellaneous

Other factors, such as adherence to the atheistic-communist ideology, Satanism, as well as conversion to other religions such as Islam, Hinduism, Sikhism, etc., have played a role in the gradual demise of European Christianity.

PART 3C

A more detailed look at the factors leading to the decline of European Christianity

In the previous chapter, I touched briefly on the factors that, in my view, have led Europeans to turn their backs on the Church of Jesus Christ, my Lord.

In the following segment, I will consider the factors in some detail.

A) Science & Technology

That insights gained from scientific research have led Europeans to abandon the Christian faith is indeed a paradox, for Christianity not only liberated the minds of Europeans from superstition, but is also credited with initiating scientific research on the continent. Indeed, medieval monks are credited with establishing universities, which brought about scientific research on the continent.

While not the leading cause for the decline of Christianity in Europe, advancement in scientific and technological knowledge has led others to erroneously think humanity is capable of using its brains to solve all our problems—outside the realm of God Almighty.

Admittedly, science and technology have advanced the material benefits of technology in our lifestyles. But have developments brought about by scientific and technological advancement made us any happier?

Has not the human mind that discovered the aeroplane employed the same technology to develop bomber jets throwing bombs around to inflict mass human casualties and inflict untold suffering on those who have a chance to survive the mayhem caused by our so-called advancement in knowledge?

As the conflict raging in Ukraine as I write these lines in mid-2022 demonstrates, our so-called scientific and technological advancement has made us even more vulnerable to obliteration through our inventions!

So what is the basis of our boasting?

We fail to realize that the core problem, the problem of the sinful heart, has not been resolved. We go to space, but we cannot even form lasting, peaceful bonds in marriage. We go to space, but we cannot control our anger leading us to murder here and there. We go to outer space, but we have not overcome our inner emptiness.

We had best get on our knees and beg the Divine to heal our wretched hearts than go about denying His existence!

The above was by way of introduction. I want to detail the three areas where scientific advancement has negatively impacted on European Christianity.

i)   The Big Bang theory

I once came across an article on the big bang theory.

The article stated that the Universe began as hot, tiny particles mixed with light and energy. The minute particles converged together to form atoms. Over time, those atoms congregated to form stars, planets, comets, asteroids, etc. According to the article, the Universe is around 13.8 billion years old.

As far as I can recall, the author failed to detail how the tiny particles he referred to emerged in the first place.

The bottom line of the Big Bang Theory is that the Universe came about by accident, yes, the collision of atoms billions of years ago. Such ideas emanating from science, though not proven, could lead others to deny the existence of a Creator God.

Suppose everything came about through an accidental big bang; then the idea of a Supernatural being who created the Universe, yes, who controls the Universe's destiny, does not make sense, does it?

Sadly, many in our day, including a considerable proportion of the European population, accept the unproven theory as fact.

Almighty God brought the universe into being. Whether it was by way of a Big Bang, a Huge Bang, or an enormous Bang is, as far as I am concerned, unimportant.

The problem begins when we start to assign the phenomena to pure accident!

Accident, *really*? And you believe that wild assertion? Please count me out. Indeed, I recognize the working of the Supernatural in the world around me!

ii) The Theory of Evolution

I watched a BBC TV documentary where a reporter visited the Congo Forest to observe the Chimps. As he gazed at these intriguing creatures in awe, he remarked: "These are our ancestors!"

As the example of the BBC reporter just cited shows, many growing up in Europe and the West, in general, are brought up to believe that humans evolved from chimpanzees—by dint of accident. This leads me to the theory of Evolution. Of course, it is beyond the realm of this book to delve into the fine details of the Evolutionary Theory. The following section represents only a nutshell of the theory:

In 1859, Charles Darwin published the book *The Origin of Species*. In it, he postulated that all plants and animals originated from bacteria-like microorganisms more than 3 billion years ago. Natural selection assisted the process of Evolution.

On their part, humans and other mammals are supposed to have emerged from shrew-like creatures that lived more than 150 million years ago.

Whereas I do not dispute some of the findings of Darwinism, I consider the conclusion that all species of life originated by chance from a common ancestor, a primordial cell and that diversity in organisms came about through natural selection and the survival of the fittest as outrageous, yes, beyond the pale.

As already mentioned, the belief in *Twediapong Nyankopong*, Almighty God, is widespread in my native society. The proposition of Evolution thus had no bearing on my belief that Almighty God created everything.

I only learnt what I was taught at school in line with the saying "chew, pour, pass and forget." After passing my exams, I threw all I learnt about Evolution into the junk bin of my brain archive.

Put in another way, the knowledge I acquired concerning the Evolution of the species did not have any bearing on my belief in God's existence.

Unfortunately, that is not the situation with children growing up in Europe and other parts of the world, particularly the western world and the communist societies.

Sticking with Western Europe, school children growing up there, many of whom have not been taught by their parents about the existence of Almighty God, are inclined to accept the postulations of the theory of Evolution as a fact, yes, an absolute truth.

Evolution, by definition, is an ongoing process, not a static one. Deducing from that insight and restricting ourselves to humanity, one would expect humans not to remain stagnant in our evolutionary process; instead, one would expect humans to continue evolving into beings endowed with different physical features from our own!

Records show humans have been on earth for several centuries.

Though they have become arrogant, boastful, self-conceited—you can go on naming the adjectives you might use to describe individuals who display excessive pride and self-satisfaction in their achievements, possessions, or abilities till the cows come home—they have nevertheless not changed or evolved physically, or spiritually.

Ouch! I just forgot to add how much modern humans like blowing their trumpets to the rest of creation! Humanity indeed keeps bragging; yes, keeps blowing its trumpet to impress upon the rest of the universe how sophisticated they have become. "We have evolved into superhumans—beings capable of ultimately settling on Mars, Jupiter, the moon and other planets of the universe." Thus they keep talking big!

As far as their physical features go, however, homo sapiens have, over the years, kept the same characteristics, yes, appearances.

Though Evolution, at best, is just a theory, a conjecture, it has been accepted by many, including the likes of the BBC reporter referred to above, as a fact, yes, an unquestionable fact.

One can imagine how difficult it is to convey the Gospel of salvation to an individual firmly entrenched in the belief of

Evolution, who holds the view that all organisms emerged millions of years ago from a primordial cell.

Strangely, some are prepared to believe an unproven theory of what might have occurred millions if not billions of years ago whilst at the same time disbelieving the accounts of the birth, ministry, death, resurrection and ascension of the Lord Jesus.

Do people of this group refuse to believe biblical teaching just because it will erode their own firmly held views on the theory of Evolution?

How can the theory of Evolution accommodate the extraordinary events associated with the earthly life of the Son of God?

Will the proponents of Evolution make others believe the Son of God also evolved from a primordial cell?

iii) Palaeontology

From time to time, palaeontologists publish, with great acclaim and bold headlines, findings that validate scientific postulations concerning how life evolved on earth.

Concerning the origins of humans, they keep changing their claims all the time.

Today one may read findings that claim humans first emerged in one part of the globe, only for the same scientist to claim a completely different location where humans were supposed to have arrived on earth.

Using their skeleton finds, they paint pictures that allegedly corroborate the fact humans came from chimpanzees.

Regarding the approximate time humans and other organisms emerged on planet earth, they resort to carbon dating techniques in their estimation. Concerning the use of that technique to estimate the age of fossil finds, I want to present the contribution of a German Christian in the matter.

I got to know him by chance. I was travelling from Hannover, where I was based, to visit a German friend resident in Calw, a town not far from Stuttgart, about three hundred kilometers to the south of Hannover where I was resident.

I didn't possess a car. I could have travelled by train or bus, but I opted instead for what in Germany is known as a *Mitfahrgelegenheit*, a hitchhiking—with a difference. Whereas one hitchhikes for free, the type I am referring to involves contacting an agency which links drivers to passengers. For a small fee, they link you to a driver, who usually charges a token fee. Apart from being cheap, it is generally considered safer than hitchhiking, especially for women, because the drivers are registered; so if something goes wrong, the driver can be traced. Today one may do it online; in those days, one had to call the office and register. It is a cheap way of travelling. So I booked a trip from Hannover to Stuttgart and travelled the remaining distance by train.

Often one would travel with up to three other passengers; on this occasion, I was the only passenger. Sometimes it takes time to develop a kind of rapport with a stranger—in this case with the driver. As far as my memory goes, a rapport happened quickly. Initially, we talked about general issues; when he got to know I shared his Christian faith, he turned the conversation to our common faith.

"Robert," he began, "let's consider the matter. Should Almighty God call into existence a tree today, right now as we are talking, you and I, who were not present, on passing by the tree tomorrow, might estimate its age as perhaps five or more years old, wouldn't we? In the sight of Almighty God, however, such a tree is just a day old.

"Furthermore, were Almighty God to call a massive mountain into existence today, those who attempt to estimate its age based on its rocks may think it is a million years old. In contrast, as far as the Creator is concerned, that mountain has just come into existence—just a day old!

"So all the thoughts of humans using carbon dating to decipher the age of the universe are pointless as far as Almighty God is concerned."

Whenever I hear the so-called experts call out huge numbers to indicate the universe's age, my thoughts go back to that conversation I had with my German Christian brother!

The problem is that whereas individuals established in the faith easily brush aside such wild conjectures and claims, someone living in a place like Europe, individuals who, as we have noted, were not brought up to believe in Creation, tend to accept the wild conjecture as truth.

We can indeed travel the world and unearth the bones of myriads of fossils buried underneath the ground. That on its own cannot erase the fact of God's existence. No, the eternal reality of God's presence cannot be done away with by insights from studying the universe created by Himself.

B) Perceived contradictions in the Bible

The sophisticated European/Western mind approaches the Bible as it often does with a book of literature, a play by Shakespeare, for example.

Such individuals scrutinize the Bible as they would an ordinary book of literature, using the academic techniques of literary criticism. They perform an exercise in critique on the Bible. As they do so, they soon discover contradictions. Such perceived contradicting and difficult-to-interpret areas in the Bible lead them to reject God. The matter is not only true of unbelievers. Some who accept the Gospel may question their faith or even abandon it due to passages in the Bible they wrestle with.

The Bible, indeed, is the inspired word of God. It should also be clear to all that Almighty God is above the Bible.

Abraham worshipped and, yes, interacted with Almighty God at a time when the Bible did not exist! Indeed, those who cite perceived Biblical inconsistencies in rejecting Almighty God should be aware that Abraham and most of the Old Testament saints walked with Almighty God when there was no Bible!!

Let us consider a hypothetical situation where fire destroys every Bible on earth. Will Almighty God cease to exist because there is no Bible to refer to?

My advice to those having difficulty with the Bible or parts of it is for them to go on their knees and implore Almighty God to touch them, yes, to open their eyes to behold the reality of His being.

One needs to pray for the Lord to come into one's life. That is the first step. Once that happens, the Lord, by His mercy and grace, will give you the needed grace to understand His word—including those parts which may appear difficult to fathom.

That has also been my experience. Indeed, before my born-again experience, I also wrestled with parts of the scripture.

That is no longer the case. That does not imply I now understand everything in the Bible. Yes, I still do not wholly comprehend everything written in the Bible. Why not? The answer is simple. The Lord declares in His word, the Bible: *"For my thoughts are not your thoughts, neither are your ways my ways, saith the Lord. For as the heavens are higher than the earth, so are my ways higher than your ways, and my thoughts than your thoughts."* Isaiah 55:8-9

Some may consider my attitude childish, immature, yes, naïve, but my faith is sufficient to stand against such criticism.

C) Perceived failings of the established church past and present

Those who want to wait until they find a perfect church to fellowship with will wait in vain. The Church is where imperfect human beings gather to worship Almighty God.

Even the most seemingly perfect, or sincere human being is not without fault.

For such an individual looking for a perfect church before accepting Christ, the Lord, this is my message:

Accepting Christ is a personal decision. Fellowship with Christ is a personal issue. It has more to do with our relationship with God and less to do with the Church.

The Church is a fellowship of believers. Indeed, for the young in the faith, the Church will help nurture faith; but ultimately, it is not the Church we attend that matters but our relationship with Christ.

In the same way, we should not allow the perceived failings of the Church to prevent us from accepting the message of the Cross.

For unbelievers and those unfamiliar with the Bible, it could be counterproductive to cite stories in the Bible in conversation about Christianity. Nevertheless, I will do precisely that at this juncture:

There is a story in the Bible where Jesus met a Samaritan woman at a well.

Being thirsty, the Lord asked the lady for a drink.

"Why are you, a Jew, requesting water from a Samaritan woman? We don't like each other, so why do you want me to give you my water?"

Next, the conversation switched to the place of worship. "You Jews want everyone to worship God in Jerusalem. On the other hand, our ancestors demanded that we worship on this mountain" (she might have pointed to it).

Jesus replied: "Neither in Jerusalem nor on this mountain do we worship God. God is a spirit, and those who worship Him should do so in spirit and in truth."

Indeed, the Lord demands that we worship Him in spirit and in truth. We should not allow the perceived failures of the church to prevent us from making the right choice, which is to accept Him into our lives.

D) The politicization of the church

The politicization of the church has not served the course of European Christianity. I want, in this regard, to cite the ongoing conflict between Catholics and Protestants in Northern Ireland. Obviously, the conflict has nothing to do with the Gospel of Salvation; yes, the Gospel, which among others, implores us to love our neighbours as ourselves, to pray for our enemies and seek reconciliation when others offend us.

For those not familiar with the teachings of the Gospel, those not firmly grounded in their faith, those already facing personal challenges with their faith, the perpetual conflicts between the Catholic and Protestant denominations, confrontations that sometimes become violent could lead them to reject Christianity.

E) Confusion concerning which religion holds the truth

In my conversation with my European friends and colleagues on faith issues, I realize there is some confusion among some Europeans regarding which faith to follow. Firstly, some are perplexed as to which Christian denomination—Catholic, Protestant, Evangelical etc. to follow. Then there is the uncertainty as to which of the religions—Christianity, Islam, Sikh, Buddhism, etc.—hold absolute truth.

In this connection, I must state some Europeans I have tried to evangelize have expressed their disquiet regarding Christianity's assertion of being the only path to Almighty God. Some have said to my face that they consider that Christian stance to be arrogant.

Today's generation of Western Europeans grew up after the tumultuous period of World War II. They have grown up in free, democratic societies. In their societies, multiple parties representing various issues, ideologies, thoughts, etc., canvass freely for adherents/members. Indeed, the democratic culture allows for pluralistic discussions, thoughts, ideas, expressions, etc. There are, for example, the social democrats fighting for the interest of workers, conservatives for business, the greens for environmental issues, etc.

In the same way, individuals are free to choose political parties based on the issues, thoughts, and programmes they campaign on; the European mindset is trained to permit free argument and encourages the same to happen in the matter of religion.

"Why should Christians claim to be the only way to God?" I have been questioned not on a few occasions. "Give everyone the right to worship whatever they choose," someone else told me.

Here is another curious observation I have made during my stay in Europe:

Over the years, immigrants have arrived in Europe from various parts of the globe—including Africa. Asia, Latin America, etc. The newcomers have brought their faiths and beliefs—multiple brands of Christianity and Islam, Judaism, Buddhism, Sikhs, etc., to Europe. The newcomers to Europe have not only brought their religious practices—Muslims, Jews, Hindus, etc.—they usually hold tenaciously to their beliefs and pass them on to their offspring.

And yet, on the contrary, their European hosts seem to have abandoned their predecessors' religion or faith.

Not established in the faith of their ancestors and in line with their commitments to the principle of religious tolerance, they allow the newcomers the freedom to practice their religions whilst theirs is in decline.

I am not saying we should prevent anyone from exercising their religious beliefs. What irritates me, however, is that by their behaviour, a section of the indigenous population seems to be advocating in favour of the newcomers' religions to the disadvantage of their own Christian heritage.

I have observed this trend, especially in England, where the English, of all people, the English, associated with the saying "my home is my castle", freely gives way to the introduction of a multitude of foreign religions. Instead of acting in the spirit of that adage and holding tenaciously to their Christian heritage, they have sadly abandoned their Christian faith. In some cases, they have sold their churches to be converted to mosques, Hindu temples, places of gathering for Sikhs, etc. Of course, I am not preaching religious intolerance. On the contrary, I am a strong advocate of religious freedom and tolerance. Indeed, I wouldn't coerce anyone into accepting my faith. But that does not mean I should abandon my faith; yes, I recognize and am aware of the decline of my religion whilst the newcomers grow theirs.

By the same token, one cannot move into a predominantly Islamic country and dictate the terms of religious worship to them; in the same way, I expect the same to happen in Europe. Sadly, that doesn't seem to be the case when it comes to matters of the faith of their fathers. Indeed, I have the impression that in a country such as the UK adherents of religions aside from Christianity have it easier than Christians.

F) The European Mindset

In my interaction with my European friends, one aspect of their thinking came to the fore. They are inclined to analyze any fact in "anatomical detail" to fish out the logic or rationale behind it before accepting it.

The typical European tends to break apart a declaration presented to him or her for the logic behind the declaration before accepting it as truth.

I read in an article that this is the legacy of the period of the Enlightenment.

Here is a brief explanation for those who may not be conversant with the term:

In the spirit of the Enlightenment legacy, Europeans tend to analyse everything to get at the truth and logic before accepting or believing it. The European mindset is inclined to seek rational, logical solutions to all issues.

Put another way; the Western mindset is based on the idea that truth can be derived through logical, rigorous debate.

Facts, logic and reason are critical to the reasoning and thinking of the average European. The enlightenment-orientated, humanistic mindset is built on the concept that individuals have absolute control over their lives and are free to behave and act in line with what is accepted within the rules set out by the secular state.

That approach may work well in the physical realm.

The problem begins, however, the moment we attempt to carry that attitude into matters related to the Divine, yes, the spiritual realm of our existence, indeed, into issues pertaining to Almighty God.

To tell Europeans with this type of mindset to accept Bible verses such as "my ways are not your ways, nor are my thoughts your thoughts" is a challenge indeed. Some may consider me naive, but I accept this biblical verse with childlike faith.

A European with a typical European mindset will be inclined to tell me to the face: "Why should I allow a supernatural being who I cannot see with my eyes to think for me? No, I am in charge of my body and life. I do what pleases me!" That attitude is typical in the post-Christian European setting.

Parental control of the individual's life ceases when the individual attains the age of 18. After attaining 18, one is considered mature and not subjected to any restrictions on one's life. The individual is permitted to do almost everything within the legal parameters of society.

The individual may choose to smoke, drink alcohol, consume drugs, engage in sex, and change as many partners as possible. Life is one's own. One can do whatever one chooses.

Ultimately, that kind of thinking could be summed up as follows: *Let us eat, drink and be merry for tomorrow we die!*

Yes, we live only once, so let us enjoy life today, for tomorrow we die. Make hay while the sun shines, as it were.

The European mindset is rooted in humanism which postulates, among others, the idea that humans do not need a god or religion to satisfy their spiritual and emotional needs.

Humanism excludes the existence of the spiritual world. The presence of God and, for that matter, Satan, does not fit into the mindset of the humanist.

The question worth asking is: does the fact that a section of humanity rejects the reality of the spiritual realm render it non-existent? Of course not!

To dismiss the existence of the spiritual realm of our existence, in my view, is like rejecting the fact that oxygen, an essential for life, is a part of the air we breathe!

I have, on several occasions, mentioned my reluctance to quote from the Bible, among others things, in order not to confuse those who are not familiar with its teachings.

I want to make an exception here: The Bible refers, in several instances, to Satan and the host of demons under his control.

Whereas Almighty God will not impose himself on the individual, yes, whereas Almighty God gives the individual a choice to either serve Him or deny Him, Satan does not adopt such a gentle attitude. Instead, He forces himself into the lives of the individual who has turned his back on his Maker.

Still, in the matter of the modern European mindset causing difficulty believing in the Christian message, I want to cite an example from the Bible to illustrate why it is difficult for the modern European mind to come to terms with the workings of Almighty God.

I cite the example of Joseph.

Joseph was serving his master. The wife of his master wanted him to commit adultery with her, but Joseph stood by the teachings of the Ten Commandments. He did what the Ten Commandments handed to the Jews on Mount Sinai demanded, one of the commandments being: "Do not commit adultery." And so Joseph ran away from the scene, putting temptation behind him.

The wife of his master subsequently reported Joseph to her husband, accusing him of attempting to rape her. Joseph was, in due course, arrested and thrown into prison.

The modern western mindset, which operates along the lines of logic, would certainly have difficulty coming to terms with such a situation, and might argue as follows:

"Almighty God, you set the rules forbidding Joseph to commit adultery. He acted precisely according to the rules; he followed your laws. Why, then, didn't you protect him, indeed, prevent his arrest and imprisonment!"

Speaking of prison life!

Friends, I have worked as a prison doctor in the UK for several years. Compared to the conditions prevailing in prisons in other parts of the world, prisons in the UK can be described as quite comfortable; even so, I would never want to be an inmate in a UK prison.

If prison life today is harsh, let us consider what it would have been like in Joseph's time. My goodness, the conditions would have been horrific.

There are several other instances of righteous suffering.

That found its climax in the crucifixion of Christ.

The western mindset, which centers on logic, would, without doubt, have great difficulty coming to terms with such a paradoxical situation. That could be a reason for Europeans to reject God.

Another example:

The Bible states in many places that God is love.

For the European mindset, the loving God should provide us with roses and not thorns, kisses and not insults. Yes, we do not want God to permit suffering of any kind to visit our homes.

For a loving God to allow human monsters like Adolf Hitler to live even a single day to commit the horrible atrocities associated with him is something the Western mindset has great difficulty coming to terms with.

I am not claiming to understand the mind of Almighty God; I also don't comprehend all his ways; I follow him in blind faith.

With faith, I accept his Word which says His ways are not mine; indeed, sometimes we have to become fools, silly, and appear to be naive to follow the Lord. That is it. He says we should behave like children and trust him through good and evil. That is, undoubtedly, something the modern mind finds difficult to accept. Well, since the Lord 'changeth not', we should accept His leading as it is.

Indeed, I admit I do not always understand some of the terrible things happening around me; but that does not lead me to abandon my faith.

Some may find it difficult to swallow; the fact remains that those who want to walk with God are advised to leave their intellect behind. Rational thinking, in human terms, will not bring us far in our walk with God. Very often a leap of Faith is necessary.

Why? The answer is simple—God's ways are not our ways. Period.

That, indeed, is the reason why many in our days experience problems with the Christian faith.

For indeed, God's ways are not our ways. I do not want to go into details, but I also have, as it were, a thorn in my flesh, a challenge involving a family member. I don't understand why it should be so, but that does not mean I am rejecting the existence of Almighty God.

Before I leave the matter of the European mindset and attitudes: I have, in the meantime, discovered a fundamental flaw in the so-called Enlightenment-orientated European thinking. I cited earlier the example of a European who stood behind a chimp and declared that chimps are our ancestors! Where is the logic here, my "sophisticated-minded European" counterpart?

You want to analyse everything for logic before accepting or believing! Where, indeed, is the logic here? If we evolved from chimps, why haven't we evolved further into something else?

I will have to end the matter here; those who wish to have further discussions on the topic may contact me later.

G) Catastrophes, sufferings, injustices, etc., in the face of a loving God

As mentioned elsewhere, the European mindset has difficulty coming to terms with a loving God who permits suffering.

Indeed, I have on several occasions when I have had conversations with my European friends on my Christian faith, met with comments like:

> "How can there be a God who, for example, permits hunger and suffering on earth, especially in your native Africa? Children are dying from hunger in Africa; how do you reconcile that with a loving and caring God?"

Of course, we should do whatever we can to alleviate suffering in the world.

Yet when I ponder on my European friends citing the suffering in other parts of the world to reject the existence of God, I recognise a curious pattern.

My friends, blessed in abundance by Heaven, cite third parties' suffering to reject God. The irony, or is it a paradox, is that those individuals who are in the hot soup are not doubting the existence of God!

Indeed, if you interview them, hardly any of them would question God's existence.

Indeed, despite their harsh conditions, many acknowledge God's existence and still worship Him; yes, they praise His name irrespective of their suffering, notwithstanding their dire situations.

Sadly, the Europeans, who should be thanking God for the blessings they enjoy, make the suffering of others a stumbling block to their faith. For them to accept an omnipotent and omnipresent God who allows suffering all around us—no thanks!

What indeed a paradox!

Yet another example: During the attack that hit Paris in November 2015, I remember reading an article a day or so later in which the writer put the question: "Where was God during the attack?"

Even as I sit in front of my laptop and write this piece, television is bringing into our homes pictures depicting the suffering others are enduring in places of conflict like Ukraine.

The havoc wreaked by the Covid-19 pandemic is undoubtedly fresh in our minds as I write this piece in November 2022.

Much as I sympathize with the general frustration concerning evil in the world, one thing remains certain: Almighty God is not dead.

He was and is and will evermore be Almighty God.

He was alive when Abraham was called to seek a new home; He was alive when His son Jesus Christ manifested Himself powerfully in the world's affairs; He is alive in all eternity.

On the matter of suffering in the world—

If we were honest with ourselves, we would acknowledge that much of the mess that has engulfed the world is of our own making, not God's.

We can also compare Almighty God with an earthly parent who has given his children the freedom to do whatever they choose based on the red lines he has set for them. He has, out of love, set out the red lines for their benefit.

Instead of staying within their boundaries, they have disobediently crossed the red lines into the danger zone. As predicted by the father, they are not faring well in the prohibited area.

Having gotten themselves into problems by disobeying their father, the children are now turning around to accuse him of not hastening quickly enough to their rescue!

H) Wars past and present

When we fail to resolve our conflicts amicably and resort to war through the use of destructive weapons produced by ourselves, humanity is quick to point fingers at the Almighty for permitting us to self-destroy ourselves!!

Let's sit down to ponder the matter again.

Our earthly parents warn us not to touch burning charcoal. We consider ourselves more intelligent than our parents and do just that. Now our fingers are burning, reaping as it were the consequences of our disobedience. Instead of exercising self-criticism, we have turned our anger on our parents, heaping insults upon them for not averting the harm caused to us!

I don't want to turn this into a forum to discuss the issue of war and the sufferings associated with it. We should do all we can to prevent wars. Wars and conflicts are, however, the symptoms and not the cause of the problem.

The cause of the problem is the evil human heart, at war with ourselves, our neighbors and ultimately with our Maker!

Let us, for example, sit down to consider the horrific war that continues to rage in Ukraine. As I sat down to watch the human misery and suffering unfolding on TV, the question that kept surfacing was—what is all the suffering for?

Couldn't the matter have been resolved amicably? If I got the reports right, Russia's main reason for starting it was its concern Ukraine would join NATO one day.

Based on the above, I am led to conclude that Russia invaded Ukraine out of fear of tomorrow.

Should the fear of tomorrow *that never comes* lead one to go to war and bring about such human suffering?

If, after we fail to resolve our misunderstandings amicably, we find ourselves in a mess, is it fair on our part to point accusing fingers at Almighty God for preventing our self-inflicted injuries?

Are we calling on Almighty God to take our free will to make decisions out of our hands and turn us into robotic machines, yes, zombies subject to His permanent control?

Speaking of the destruction brought by wars—the question that comes to mind is: who developed the weapons of war in the first place? Our fallen nature is the cause of wars. But let us sit down to ponder the matter. Assuming wars were fought only with our human strength, resorting to our heads (headbutting), hands (blows) and legs (kicking), could we inflict great harm to our opponents?

Of course not; instead, we would have been able to cause only limited harm to our foes.

But no! The human heart running from its Maker, capable of doing good and evil, has come up with weapons and implements capable of inflicting untold suffering on others.

To start with, we came up with crude instruments of destruction—stones, clubs, bows, arrows, etc.

Still burning in our desire to inflict even more damage on our foes, we developed simple guns, crude guns. No, the simple guns do not carry enough destructive power, we said to ourselves.

So we designed more powerful guns—revolvers, machine guns, assault rifles, etc.

In due course we added biological, chemical, and nuclear weapons; yes, we added weapons capable of human annihilation into our weapon arsenal. Having used the free will at our disposal to amass weapons instead of, for example, alleviating poverty, we are now going about insulting Almighty God, yes, dragging His Name in the mud for the destruction and the suffering brought about by our human-made weapons!

It is difficult to discuss the very foundations of the problem with a European already battling to believe in God in the first place. But the core of the matter is that when Almighty God created the universe at the beginning, all was good. That evil came about because of the rebellion of Satan.

Indeed wars, famine and all the suffering cannot undermine the fundamental issue of the existence of Almighty God. It is my prayer that the Holy Spirit of the living God will penetrate the heart of anyone struggling to believe, so they may come to see the light.

I) Poverty among those worshipping God

I have, on several occasions, had conversations about my faith in Christ with those who have difficulties believing in Him.

The arguments such individuals present to explain their rejection of the Gospel can be summed up as the following: "If your people in Africa spend a good deal of their time worshipping God and He does not help you sort out the myriads of problems besetting your continent—poverty, hunger, diseases, etc., why do you want to recommend Him to me/us?"

Unfortunately, many African migrants to Western Europe and the rest of the Western World seem to be influenced by such arguments!

If Europeans who brought the Gospel to Africa have turned their backs on it, why should I be bothered?

Such arrivals to Europe from Africa have either abandoned their faith or, at best, become lukewarm Christians. The fire that was aglow in them when in Africa has either grown dim or has become wholly extinguished.

On the surface, such an argument may seem plausible and logical.

That is, however, not the way Almighty God operates. The human mind, for example, reasons on the lines of 2 plus 2 equals 4. Well, though I do not claim to occupy the office of Speaker for Almighty God, based on studying His Word and observing His workings in my life, that is not how things operate with our Heavenly Father. His ways are not our ways, His logic, not our logic!

Indeed, such reasoning misses the point; namely, the existence of God Almighty does not depend on our personal, national or continental fortunes.

Instead, it boils down to the individual inviting Him into their lives, inviting Him to accompany them on their respective journeys along life's rugged paths.

J) Difficulty coming to terms with the concept of Satan, demons, principalities

As I mentioned elsewhere, I grew up in a society in which the belief in the supernatural is widespread. In the same way, all in the population believe in God; and also believe in evil forces—Satan, demons, witches, etc.

Europeans I have interacted with not only have problems believing in God but also do likewise with the concept of the evil forces of darkness—Satan, demons, witches, etc. For many Europeans, whatever is not scientifically validated is rejected.

K) Humanistic worldview

Observing European society first-hand for over forty years has brought a realization home to me:

In Western European society, the general thinking is that life is one's own, so one can do whatever one wishes with one's life. "It is my life. I have the freedom to do whatever I wish with it", is the general thinking.

When they reach 18, individuals consider themselves liberated, emancipated from whatever minor restrictions on their lives were being imposed on them by their parents or guardians, as the case may be. At that stage, they consider themselves free to do whatever they choose with their lives, independent of any controls, human or Divine.

To bring home the message of Christianity, yes, the idea of them having to submit to a Supernatural Power, Almighty God, is not palatable to the ears of a modern-day European. That, indeed, is the impression I have had; others may of course disagree with me on the matter.

L) Prosperity and the European Welfare State System

Though it should not cause someone to lose faith in God, wealth tends to do just that.Growing up in our little village's impoverished settings, I could hear my mother earnestly pleading in an almost daily basis with Almighty God to provide her with the means to feed her children.

If through mysterious circumstances, she managed to feed her children at the end of the day, she gave thanks to the Supreme Being for His kindness.

When I was resident in Ghana in the 1970s, the country was in economic turmoil. There were times when I was almost penniless. Whenever I got up in the morning, I prayed to Heaven to provide me with the means to feed myself on that particular day. It was living from hand to mouth, one day at a time.

The situation changed when I moved to Europe. Even though I did not deem myself part of the wealthy members of society, I obtained my daily bread without much ado.

Concerning my Christian faith, whereas I was fasting and praying regularly in my native Ghana, I found it challenging to maintain this routine in Europe. Slowly but surely, my faith was growing cold. Thank God I have nevertheless been able to keep my faith through His grace.

That leads me to one of the causes that, in my view, has led to the decline in Christianity in Europe.

Europe, Western Europe in particular, has grown wealthy over the years. Many countries have a generous welfare state system to care for those who fall through the social network.

Those unemployed are entitled to state benefits that pay for accommodation, food, healthcare and other basics.

Since the state is there to cater generously for me, why do I need to look up to a Power I cannot see for assistance?

Such blessed individuals should be doing precisely that—showing their gratitude to their Creator for sparing them some of the harsh living conditions to which some are subject in other parts of the world.

Sadly, that is not the case. Instead, in some instances, wealth has led some to become self-conceited. In their false pride and exaggerated sense of self-importance, they have the audacity not only to disbelieve in Almighty God, but to look down on all who do so.

As already indicated, multiple factors have led to the decline of the church in Europe—and wealth no doubt counts among them.

M) Social Media

The gradual decline of European Christianity set in long before the advent of social media.

The flame of European Christianity began to grow dim, indeed was threatened with extinction long before the internet came into being.

Social media can thus not be assigned blame for the sad state of the Religion of Jesus Christ, King of Kings and Lord of Lords on the European continent.

Social media has, however, aggravated an already dire situation. The other day as I went on my doctor's rounds in the prison where I was working, a prisoner on constant watch due to the threat of suicide pleaded with me to administer a lethal injection to end it all for him!

Social Media, you might say, has been injecting the lethal injection into the gravely ill European Christianity to put it to bed—forever!

Individuals who already have no connection with Almighty God, yes, who have given up on their faith, may find a false sense of hope in the virtual world. This is especially true of the youth.

In a society where children learn from infancy about the existence of God, they usually become grounded in their faith. Later, they become less susceptible to social pressure or other influencers to abandon their faith. The situation is different for those who have not had that opportunity.

Since European youth are generally not brought up to believe in God, they are prone to be led astray by so-called online influencers.

Even those with a nominal belief in God may spend an inordinate amount of time with Facebook, You Tube, or Instagram, leaving them little time for Bible reading or study.

N) Miscellaneous

So far, I have touched on some factors that have led to the decline of European Christianity. The list, no doubt, is incomplete. Other factors, such as adherence to the atheistic-communist ideology, Satanism, as well as conversion to other religions such as Islam, Hinduism, Sikhism, etc., have played a role in the gradual demise of European Christianity.

PART 4

Effects of rejection of Christ by Europe

Post-Christian Europe like a ship without anchor

Having dwelt on the path of European Christianity from the point of its introduction to the continent, the initial challenges it encountered by way of persecution, the conversion of Emperor Constantine that led to the adoption of Christianity as the official religion of the continent, Europe's influential role in missionary activities, the factors that have led to the decline of Christianity on the continent, I now turn to consider the impact the rejection of the Christian message has had on European society.

On the surface, one would think the rejection of the Gospel has not adversely impacted on European society. Europe has attained a high infrastructural development. The cities, towns and even rural areas are generally well developed, boasting all the amenities that bring comfort to modern-day life.

Multi-party democracy has brought liberties others yearn for elsewhere. Things really work in Europe. Citizens go about their lives quite peacefully.

Indeed, new arrivals in Europe would be led to think they have arrived in a kind of heaven on earth, where the populace is enjoying a high standard of living; yes, enjoying prosperity in peace and tranquillity. I thought precisely along those lines when I first stepped onto the soil of Europe.

Indeed, when I first stepped on the soil of Western Europe, on the grounds of West Berlin to be precise and beheld the beautiful scenery of wonderful modern houses, broad roads filled with traffic made up of vehicles in top condition, the neatly dressed, well-fed residents going about their activities, I thought I had landed in paradise, indeed the promised land.

It wouldn't take long, though, for it to dawn on me that that was not the case. Indeed, whereas things appeared on the surface to be in good order, I realized there were deep-seated societal problems related in particular to the mental health of the populace.

The first incident that challenged my presumption of a society where the citizenry lived in comfort and absolute satisfaction with their lives happened only a few weeks into my stay. It involved the case of a young German man who was instantly killed after deliberately jumping in front of a moving train in an act of suicide.

Not long after that tragic happening, the story of a middle-aged woman who made a desperate call for donations to pay for her dog's surgery made headlines in the city.

"If my dog dies, I will die!" was the headline of the front-page story carried by a leading boulevard newspaper. The individual in the report explained that she lived alone with her dog. The dog was her only companion, so there would be no point in living without it.

Both incidents gave me food for thought. It came home to me that the Europeans were not as happy with their lives as I initially thought.

Having lived over forty years in Europe and having inter-acted with Europeans, especially Germans and the British, such cases, heart-wrenching as they are, do not come as a surprise to me.

Why not, one may ask? My answer is that many European citizens have erroneously believed that we can centre our lives around material things and still find peace and satisfaction! Whereas material things may bring temporary satisfaction, they cannot, yes they are incapable of offering lasting peace and satisfaction.

Indeed, many Europeans have turned their backs on Christianity, the faith of their ancestors that provides stability in an unstable world. Instead, they crave happiness from things of this world and pursue contentment from the material spheres of our existence. That such an attitude will eventually lead to a personal crisis can only be a matter of time.

Why? The answer is simple—life is not confined only to the material; it also has an essential spiritual component that needs to be nourished.

One can compare individuals seeking satisfaction solely from the physical realm of their existence with a ship without an anchor. Indeed, in the same way a ship needs an anchor to withstand the storms, we need a spiritual anchor to withstand the vicissitudes of life.

That is what the Lord Jesus Christ offers— the stability needed to keep us settled in the unsettled waters of life.

* * *

Before I delve deeper into the effect of Europe's turning its back on Christianity in their society, I want to pause to introduce Christianity and briefly outline what Christianity is all about.

Indeed, one will better be able to deduce what its rejection can lead to after one has understood what Christianity stands for.

A hundred years ago Christianity's basic concept and teachings will have been familiar to the average European, even to those who did not ascribe to the faith. That is no longer the case. Today it is an open secret that the Bible plays hardly any role in the lives of many Europeans; some may even have difficulty naming even one of the twelve disciples of Christ!

That does not surprise me personally; indeed, interacting with many Europeans, especially the youth, has led me to believe many are unfamiliar with the basic teachings of the Bible. Some might indeed have been baptised as children and may even have a Bible on the bookshelves at home; however, they might never have read even one chapter from it.

So what, in a nutshell, is Christianity?

Christianity grew out of Judaism, the religion of the Israelites.

Like Judaism, Christianity teaches that Almighty God created the universe—heaven and earth. As a climax of His creation, He created Adam and Eve. He placed them in the Garden of Eden with the instruction that they can eat every fruit in the Garden except the fruit of the tree of life.

Initially, Adam and Eve kept God's instructions. Their obedience to the Lord would not last forever, however. In time the snake lured them into eating the forbidden fruit. As a consequence of their disobedience, Almighty God expelled the pair from the Garden of Eden.

Over time God chose Abraham and blessed him, promising He would bless the whole world through his seed. The descendants of Abraham later became the nation of Israel. God manifested Himself to humankind through his dealings with Israel.

Eventually, Almighty God promised to send a Messiah to rescue His people, the Jews, from bondage and oppression.

Christians believe Jesus Christ is the promised Messiah, who leads sinful humanity back to Almighty God.

The New Testament of the Christian Bible contains an account of His Life and deeds on earth.

Jesus Christ was crucified. Three days after His burial, He was resurrected back to Life. Forty days after His resurrection, he ascended into Heaven in the presence of a large gathering of His disciples.

The Holy Spirit was poured down from Heaven shortly after His ascension. The Holy Spirit empowers His disciples to overcome their sinful nature and deal with the challenges that come their way on a fallen and imperfect planet.

Christians regard the Bible as the inspired Word of God.

It is strictly not a book; it is rather a library of 66 books written by 40 authors.

The Bible contains essential teachings, principles, directives, commands, etc., on ways to a godly life.

Some of the central teachings are in the Ten Commandments in the Old Testament.

In the New Testament, the Gospels reproduce some of the teachings of the Lord Jesus. Finally, the epistles, or letters, were written mainly by the apostle Paul.

As already indicated, the Bible contains the core teachings of Christianity. I believe the Bible can be regarded as the "Christian Constitution" where the core belief of the Gospel is the promise of Jesus Christ to grant eternal life to whoever accepts Him as their saviour, expressed in the well-known words from the King James Version of the Gospel of St John 3:15-17:

*For God so loved the world, that he gave his only begot-
ten Son, that whosoever believeth in him should not
perish, but have everlasting life. For God sent not his
Son into the world to condemn the world; but that the
world through him might be saved.*

In the same way that a country only functions well when
the principles enshrined in its Constitution are adhered to, the
Church of Christ, which stands for a community of believers
in Christ, has to abide by the teachings of the Bible, yes the
"Constitution" of the Church if it is to function correctly.

It is only when the principles of the Constitution, yes, the
Bible, are adhered to that the church can stand out in society,
yes, make a difference in the world.

In former times, European societies generally regarded the
teachings of the Bible as the yardstick by which one measured
the norms of society. That does not imply everyone lived by its
teachings. Nevertheless, the teachings of the Biblical were not
challenged or put into question by society.

In post-Christian Europe, where a good portion of society
either does not possess a Bible or, if they do, hardly reads it,
the Bible's teachings are either not known or disregarded by a
sizeable proportion.

Without exaggeration, one can say that the Bible's teachings are trampled underfoot in today's post-Christian European
society.

Not only that, as underlined in my conversation with the
physiotherapist, those who dare read their Bibles in public or
express their Christian opinions publicly risk ridicule, mockery
and scorn. The consequences may be even more severe, as seen
in the case of the nurse who politely asked to pray for a patient:

one could even face the threat of job loss by publicly expressing one's Christian faith.

So, how has the rejection of Christianity impacted on the individual and society at large?

Biblical teachings on creation rejected

The Bible declares boldly in Genesis 1:1: "In the beginning God created the heaven and the earth."

Earlier in my presentation, I mentioned that in my native Ghana, there is an overwhelming belief in *Twedeampong Nyakopong* among Christians and non-Christians alike.

Thus in my native Ghana, the overwhelming majority, Christians and non-Christians alike, can live with the above declaration of the Bible.

The situation is different in modern Europe. Indeed, in post-Christian Europe, only a minority of residents believe in the Bible's declaration.

In the chapter where I discussed the factors that have led many Europeans to turn their backs on Christianity, I stated that many Europeans seem to hold to the tenets of the Big Bang theory, which has it that the universes came about accidentally through an explosion known as a Big Bang. The emergence of the universe was followed later by the accidental emergence of species, as postulated by Charles Darwin and others.

Earlier in my presentation, I cited the case of an individual who stood near a gorilla and declared, "these are our ancestors!"

Many Europeans think along those lines; yes, statistics show that a sizable proportion of modern Europeans reject the Biblical teaching on creation, that Almighty God created the universe.

If the fact of a Supreme Power, Almighty God, being the creator of the universe, is rejected by post-Christian Europe, how can one expect them to abide by the teachings of the Bible, which points to Him? That is exactly what is observed in post-Christian European societies.

As might be expected, these new ideas of the emergence of the Universe and the life entailed in it are conveyed to the next generation.

The theory of Evolution, yes, the alleged accidental emergence of life on earth, on our planet earth, which came about following an accidental big bang, is taught in schools and universities as if it were a proven fact.

Fairness would expect that school children or university students would be given the opportunity to learn the other side of the story, yes that they would be taught the Creation story as well. That, however, is not the case.

So school children and students are taught at a young age to believe the lie that humans developed by chance from apes.

Biblical teachings on sexuality and marriage rejected

I want to dwell for a moment on the Creation story as presented in Genesis.

In Genesis 1:27 we read:

So God created mankind in his own image, in the image of God he created them; male and female he created them.

One would expect a post-Christian society that does not accept the Biblical teaching as binding in their lives to reject such a statement.

That, precisely, is what one observes in post-Christian Europe, mainly Western Europe.

The Bible, which, as we have established, is rejected by post-Christian Europe, teaches that God created "male and female".

Whereas in previous times, the fact that there are two sexes, male and female, was not called into question, that is no longer the case in a post-Christian society. Indeed, in post-Christian societies, in which the teachings of the Bible are not held sacrosanct, that fundamental statement by the Bible is brought into question.

Indeed, in post-Christian Europe, gender has replaced the term sex, which initially referred to the two biological sexes, male and female.

In most post-Christian societies, anyone can choose the gender they want to be identified with.

In other words, an individual who is female today may decide to change to male the next day. The matter does not end there. Some change from male to female today only to change their minds along the way and request to be changed back to the original state!

Still staying with the Biblical account of Creation:

So the man gave names to all the livestock, the birds in the sky and all the wild animals. But for Adam no suitable helper was found. So the Lord God caused the man to fall into a deep sleep; and while he was sleeping, he took one of the man's ribs and then closed up the place with flesh. Then the Lord God made a woman from the rib he had taken out of the man, and he brought her to the man. The man said, "This is now bone of my bones and flesh of my flesh; she shall be called 'woman,' for she was taken out of man."

> *That is why a man leaves his father and mother
> and is united to his wife, and they become one flesh.*
> Genesis 2:20-24

What does post-Christian Europe make of such a provision
in the Bible?

I don't want to serve as their mouthpiece. My interactions
with several of them over the years lead me to think this would
be the likely reaction of a good proportion of them to the Biblical
teaching:

> "Not for us, my dear one. Why should anyone expect us
> to abide by provisions we no longer consider relevant?
> "Our ancestors, whose minds were unsophisticated
> and non-illuminated, adhered to those archaic provisions.
> Not for us; our minds are liberated from mental slavery,
> yes, from the mental bondage which invented a supernat-
> ural being to worship and adore. We are post-Christian
> and sophisticated. We have developed aeroplanes; we
> have deciphered the DNA; we build tunnels under the
> ocean floor to create land passages between countries;
> we send humans into space. Your archaic thinking is not
> for us."

So in Post-Christian Europe, marriage is no longer regarded
as a union between male and female as taught in the Bible.
Instead, in post-Christian Europe liberated from the bondage of
what is considered the mental slavery of Christianity, several
forms of marriage unions are making their rounds.

The saying has it "ladies first", so I will consider it from a
ladies' point of view, to begin with.

Well, in post-Christian Europe, we may have a union of female and female, female and male, male and male, and miscellaneous.

Concerning males, the following constellations are possible: Males and males; males and females and miscellaneous.

Someone may want to know what type of union is associated with the category of 'miscellaneous'—well, several constellations, the details of which I shall spare the reader.

If only post-Christian Europe, having abandoned Christian faith and Christian ethics, would let things stay as they are. But no! Having thrown their Christian faith overboard, they are going about propagating their post-Christian lifestyle to the rest of the world.

There is a saying that money talks. Yes, armed with the influential media outlets the likes of the BBC, Euro News, CNN, Post-Christian Europe and the Western world in general are going about spreading their post-Christian moral ethics to the rest of the world.

Indeed, having said goodbye to the Bible and Christian teaching on matters of marriage, sex and other moral ethics, they are going about spreading their views aggressively. Having moved the goal post in their societies, post-Christian Europe is going about aggressively spreading its morals, virtues, and ethics, yes, worldview to other parts of the world, demanding that everyone follows suit. Those who dare oppose them are branded intolerant, bigots, hate preachers, acting against the human rights of others, etc.

Post-Christian Europe is not only targeting individuals that resist their new moral codes. Indeed, countries, yes nation states that seem to pass legislations contrary to their new post-Christian moral ethics, could face sanctions, yes financial sanctions. If that is not a form of bullying on their part, what is?

Interestingly they look out for the weakest links, the poor countries of Africa and the rest of the developing world, while not daring to confront rich and influential Muslim countries who hold to social norms that conflict with theirs!

It is extraordinary that Europe that is going about propagating the concept of free speech is not permitting others to express their civilized opinions on such matters; that is indeed extraordinary.

Sometimes, one risks being prosecuted just by speaking one's mind. Yes, in some Western societies, expressing one's opinion in a civilized manner on contentious issues such as single-sex marriage could lead to prosecution on the grounds of hate speech

What a paradox—or might one say ironic?—in the European context, that a society that habitually goes about lecturing others on liberal democracy and the freedom of speech, should dogmatically promote its views and inhibit criticism of its lifestyle. By their behaviour, they seem to leave the impression that they uphold the freedom of speech as long as no one dares challenge their lifestyles. On the other hand, let anyone dare say anything considered intolerant by them in matters of sexuality, marriage, or LGBT+, and lo and behold, their much-acclaimed tolerance evaporates into thin air!

They appear self-conceited. The fact that they have made some progress, which at the end of the day could be traced to the efforts of Christian monks who set up universities, has even led them to want to play God!

They are not only against the commands of the Almighty, but whoever keeps them is frowned upon; yes, whoever dares not swim on their tide is in danger of their sanctions.

Family breakdown

The Bible teaches that God created male and female and blessed them to procreate and populate the world. Christianity advocates marriage between male and female which lasts 'till death do us part'. I am not here to present myself as a moral authority. There are two issues here, though. First, to accept the Biblical teaching as binding on our lives, to strive to abide by the rules and end up falling short of expectations due to our inherent weaknesses; second, to reject the teaching outright and do whatever we deem fit with our lives.

I am not speaking for Almighty God, but from my layman's perspective of the Bible, I believe our Lord Jesus came to the world to save sinners.

This leads me to think that if one makes the best effort to stick to the provisions of marriage as set out by the Bible and, in the end, falls short of the mark and approaches the loving heavenly Father with a contrite heart to beg for forgiveness, He will forgive the individual.

I recognize the second option in operation in post-Christian Europe.

Yes, in Post-Christian societies, where the majority have turned their backs on the Bible, such teachings are rejected outright.

"Not with us!" they might state. "Life is our own. Our bodies are our own; we are free to do whatever we consider proper with our bodies. No, we refuse to permit any perceived Supernatural Authority to dictate how we should lead our lives."

In line with that thinking, the average residents of post-Christian Europe feel free to choose their partners and exchange them at will. Unrestrained in their freedom to do whatever they wish with their bodies, they may partner with a same-sex individual today, an opposite tomorrow, a combination of either later, etc., and change them at will in time.

So marriages that sometimes are sealed with much pomp, pageantry and fanfare end up a few years later, if not in a matter of months, on the dustheap—breaking apart in much acrimony.

I am not implying that broken marriages are a peculiarity of Europe.

Of course, the institution is under strain and threat in other parts of the world. I am restricting myself to Europe for reasons already referred to above.

So, family breakdowns continue to soar to the high heavens in post-Christian Europe. Sadly, it is not only the individuals concerned who suffer from the emotional turmoil of the break-up, but the children of these folk who eventually suffer under the devastating crash of the parental bond.

Statistics show children growing up in broken homes are more vulnerable to suffering under the vicissitudes of life in a troubled world than those who grow up in homes where parents live together in harmony.

It is beyond the remit of this book to discuss the issue in further detail.

Mental Health Crisis

It is generally agreed that there is an epidemic of mental health crises in Europe and the rest of the Western World.

There is indeed an epidemic of mental illness—anxiety disorder and depression on the European continent. Whereas in former times, such problems were restricted mainly to the adult population, even young children are plagued with mental health disorders these days.

To illustrate this I shall quote from a BBC News Online statement, published on July 9, 2022:

"Nearly half a million more adults in England are now taking antidepressants compared with the previous year, according to NHS figures. The number of prescriptions for children and teenagers has also risen.

During 2021-22, there was a 5% rise in the number of adults receiving antidepressants—from 7.9 million in the previous 12 months to 8.3 million.

It was the sixth year in a row that there had been an increase in both patients and prescriptions.

An estimated 83.4 million antidepressant drug items were prescribed between 2021 and 2022, which marks a 5% increase from the previous year.

There was also a rise of just over 8% in young-sters taking the medication too—from 10,994 to 11,878 among 10- to 14-year-olds; and from 166,922 to 180,455 in the 15- to 19-year-old bracket."

Before I comment on the matter, I want first to express my deep sympathy to those suffering from depression.

It is indeed a paradoxical situation. One would have expected that materially wealthy Europe would be populated by happy humans, free of anxiety, worry, and concerns about this and that.

Personally, I am not surprised by the current state of affairs.

On the one hand, we live in a world which is increasingly filled with sad and depressing news. We just came out of the COVID-19 pandemic with the associated heart-breaking news of death and suffering, only to be ushered into another crisis, the Russian invasion of Ukraine and the related suffering depicted on TV. The war indirectly affects us with the rising cost of fuel, gas, and other amenities and services.

We have become increasingly accessible to the bad news—through technology (TV, iPhones, mobile phones, laptops. etc.).

On the other hand, we have developed into a society which increasingly has drifted away from the faith of their fathers, which has negated religion and in effect cancelled out the reality of Almighty God, in whom the Bible states we could find solace in the midst of the turbulences around us.

While not saying in so many words that the depressive state of Europe today has come about solely as a result of it having turned its back on the Gospel, this factor has surely played a role.

When, on one occasion, I returned to my native Ghana on a visit, I paid a visit to a niece living in the countryside. As a single mother, she had six children aged between a few months and 14 years to feed—without any state support, I should stress.

"How are you mastering the challenging situation?" I asked.

She smiled and pointed to the high heavens. "The Lord is our shepherd; we shall not want."

Indeed, faced with a challenging situation which could have blown the minds of others apart, she was beaming with joy and counting on heavenly help.

My friend Gottfried, a retired German pastor, had a similar story to tell. On his return from Cameroon, he told me he was awe-stricken to see many individuals beaming with joy on the streets. Quite the contrary, when I sit on an underground train in Hannover, I see mainly faces that look anxious and depressed, he stated.

Mother always prayed to heaven to help us through challenges. This has nothing to do with religion being the opium of the masses. It has all to do with the recognition that there is a spiritual aspect to our existence that we cannot deny.

Many Europeans have, with a stroke of the pen, as it were, cancelled the existence of the supernatural realm—at least from their existence! They are inclined to think that because science has been able to do this and that, the spiritual realm of our existence has disappeared overnight.

Just imagine it—individuals who arrived on our planet only a few decades ago, on their own cancelling the records of the Bible pointing to the working of the supernatural!

My observation, some may disagree with me, is that the turning of the European population away from Christianity has aggravated the mental health woes of the general population.

I am not turning this presentation into a sermon. Still, I ask for your patience while I quote once again the words of our Lord Jesus Christ himself. In the Sermon on the Mount, the Lord Jesus Christ had this to tell His followers:

"Therefore I tell you, do not worry about your life, what you will eat or drink; or about your body, what you will wear. Is not life more than food, and the body more than clothes? Look at the birds of the air; they do not sow or reap or store away in barns, and yet your heavenly Father feeds them. Are you not much more valuable than they? Can any one of you by worrying add a single hour to your life?

"And why do you worry about clothes? See how the flowers of the field grow. They do not labour or spin. Yet I tell you that not even Solomon in all his splendour was dressed like one of these. If that is how God clothes the grass of the field, which is here today and tomorrow is thrown into the fire, will he not much more clothe you— you of little faith? So do not worry, saying, 'What shall we eat?' or 'What shall we drink?' or 'What shall we wear?' For the pagans run after all these things, and your heavenly Father knows that you need them. But seek first his kingdom and his righteousness, and all these things will be given to you as well. Therefore do not

*worry about tomorrow, for tomorrow will worry about
itself. Each day has enough trouble of its own. Matthew
6: 25-34 (NIV)*

Be not anxious about tomorrow, for tomorrow will take care
of itself.

How many thousands of Europeans going about plagued
with anxiety, depression, and the fear of tomorrow are at all
aware of these reassuring words of the Lord?

Someone may tell me it is fake news. To such, I will only
reply; how do you know it is fake news when you have not
tried it?

When I speak with some of my European patients plagued
with anxiety and worries, I shake my head in disbelief. Are you
anxious and apprehensive over this and that?

How I wish I could point such individuals to the Great
Burden bearer!

The matter is not straightforward, however. I mentioned earlier how a nurse who politely asked to pray for a patient was
suspended from her job and investigated.

Sadly, sharing your faith in a civilized, non-coercive manner
could get one into trouble.

Prescribe chemicals that work in the brain and provide tem-
poral relief—yes, but inviting them politely to consider accepting
the Lord as their Lord and Saviour, no!

So multitudes of Europeans have turned their backs on the
faith of their ancestors. Yes, many a good proportion of Europeans
have turned their backs on the faith of Christian giants such as
Martin Luther and Charles Wesley.

They are like plants without roots.

One could compare them with boats without a human crew
floating on the turbulent ocean waves, driven here and there,

following the waves' directions. Today, they find solace in sexual gratification only to realize a few weeks later it does not provide the needed inner peace. They move on to the next source of gratification—alcohol, and then gambling. On they go, trying one pursuit of happiness after the other—to no avail.

Ouch! Perhaps social media will provide the elusive peace. So they turn to—Facebook, Twitter, WhatsApp, Instagram, LinkedIn, you can go on naming them—still without finding peace. Ultimately, they end up where they started from, back to square one, back to their miserable state of hopelessness.

Subtle persecution of Christians

Before I leave the discussion on how Europe's turning back on Christianity has affected European society, I want to highlight briefly one curious development.

As might be expected, not everyone in Europe has turned their backs on Christianity. Yes, for sure, a sizeable proportion of the population still ascribes to the teachings of Christ.

The saying has it that the majority carries the vote. In several European countries, Christians form the minority of the population. If only the majority would leave the minority in peace to practice their faith—but this is not always the case.

With a few exceptions, the prevailing democratic system in Europe is multi-party democracy based on the principle that the majority carries the vote.

The result is that the populace, the majority of whom do not feel bound by the teachings of the Bible, elect into power parliamentarians who generally reflect the thinking of the general population.

Since Christian teachings do not bind the majority of the populace, indeed, since the majority reject the teachings of the Bible on various issues, including those about sexuality and marriage and families, the non-Christians on not a few occasions enact legislations which in some instances go against the beliefs of the Christian minority.

Those who stick to their conscience against the popular social trend are looked down upon with scorn, and are even ridiculed by the rest of society. Even worse, in some instances, they risk sanctions in the form of fines or even prison sentences!

What I am about to express is not imaginary, and no exaggeration. In some Western societies, expressing one's opinion in a civilized manner on contentious issues such as single-sex marriage could lead to prosecution on the grounds of discrimination, defamation, hate speech and what have you.

So, not only are Europeans turning their backs on the Gospel; the atmosphere is even turning hostile towards those who dare believe and express fundamental principles enshrined in the Bible.

I will need volumes to write about all the effects the rejection of the Good News of the Gospel has had on European society.

I may have to return to the matter at a future date; for now, however, I will leave the issue to rest.

PART 5

Thoughts and Prayers

What then is the way forward?

The Bible states in Hebrews 13:8:

Jesus Christ is the same yesterday and today and forever.

Jesus Christ never changes. Almighty God is the same forever. Since the Lord Jesus Christ is the same yesterday, today, and forever, yes, the creator of Heaven and Earth never changes; the moment a society that used to call itself Christian begins to use the term 'post-Christian' to refer to itself, something, without doubt, is profoundly amiss with that society.

What, indeed, has led to the current situation in Europe? Did the people of Europe search the scriptures properly? Or, in their haste to satisfy their material needs, did they fail to search the scripture with the required diligence?

One might compare the situation with a father resting in the garden of their home, sending his little boy to fetch his mobile phone from his writing desk. Just before the little boy sets out, the gate to their home opens. In enters his best friend, John:

"Come on, Jack, let's go play football!"
"Oh, that's great; wait a moment; I will be back soon."

He dashes into the building.

Moments later, he is back empty-handed.

"I did not find any phone, Dad."

"I left it there; I am a hundred per cent sure. Did you look carefully?"

"Yes, I did."

"Sure?"

"Yes."

"Go look again, boy!"

Instead of doing as required, Jack signals to his friend to follow him. Moments later, both take to their heels and dash out of the house.

"Hey, Jack, are you refusing to follow my instructions?" his father calls after him

"I don't have the time; you go fetch it yourself!" the youngster cries back.

Dad has no choice but to do precisely that. And lo and behold, he found the phone, lying in one corner of the writing desk! In his haste, little Jack had overlooked it.

The same can be said of post-Christian Europe. For whatever reason, they have not looked properly, leading them to turn their backs on the good news of the Cross.

The good thing is that there is still time for them to make amends. However, they should not behave like little Jack and run away from the message. They should instead heed the advice to go back and search, for indeed, whoever searches will find.

Yes, the only way forward for post-Christian European society is a return to the faith of their ancestors, yes, for them to re-embrace Christianity.

How can we expect Europe to re-embrace Christianity when its populace has no idea of it; yes, when according to statistics, only a tiny percentage of the populace reads the Bible regularly, and yes, when only an insignificant proportion of the population is familiar with the message of the Cross.

Earlier in my presentation I touched upon the vital role European missionaries played in spreading the Gospel around the globe. It is now time for Christians elsewhere to undertake the mission to re-evangelize Europe.

Christians worldwide should resort to all possible avenues—street evangelization, radio, social media outlets, TV, etc. in a combined mission to re-evangelize Europe.

Yes, Christians worldwide should make a concerted effort to rekindle the flame of Christianity in the "Old Continent."

The aspiring European missionary should, however, take note of some peculiar obstacles they have to deal with in their bid to spread the good news on the continent.

Earlier in my presentation, I referred to the European mind-set, which, as I pointed out, is inclined to rationalize.

As I stated earlier, I want to desist from quoting from the Bible, aware some of my readers might never have read from it.

For the final time, however, I beg the reader to permit me to quote a passage from Scripture:

People were bringing little children to Jesus for him to place his hands on them, but the disciples rebuked them. When Jesus saw this, he was indignant. He said to them, "Let the little children come to me, and do not hinder them, for the kingdom of God belongs to such as these. Truly I tell you, anyone who will not receive the kingdom of God like a little child will never enter it." And he took the children in his arms, placed his hands on them and blessed them. Mark 10: 13-16 (NIV)

As the above scripture indicates, we are called upon to accept the Gospel like little children. Therein lies the challenge for the sophisticated European mindset, which, as stated above, is inclined to analyze the facts presented for their logical truth before accepting them.

As I pointed out earlier, hardly anyone questions the existence of the supernatural in my native Ghana. The Christian missionary out to preach the Gospel on the streets of the capital Accra is unlikely to be confronted with someone who will dispute the existence of God.

Those they attempt to win for Christ may reject the message on the grounds they don't want to be associated with their church; they have their own religion, but not on the grounds of disbelief in God's existence.

The situation is very different in a typical European setting.

Indeed, a person wishing to evangelize in Europe has first to overcome a few layers, yes, deal with a few hurdles peculiar to the European ethos.

The first layer to penetrate is the concept of God. The question may indeed sound strange to the ears of an individual who grew up in a society in which the existence of God is hardly called into question, but such a question is not unexpected in the European context.

Indeed, the sophisticated European mindset which tends to demand explanation for almost everything may tend also to demand a physical proof, yes, a tangible explanation or evidence for the existence of God.

If one manages to come up with the proper arguments/ explanations to convince the European about the existence of God, another obstacle, which I will term the "Why Jesus?" question, soon comes to the fore.

"Good, you have convinced me about God's existence," they might say. "The question I have for you, though, is, why Jesus? Why not Mohammed, or Buddha or Confucius, for example?"

Indeed, many liberal-minded Europeans would be inclined to reject the claim of Christianity as being the only way that leads to God. Why not Islam, for example? It's an argument I keep hearing.

That is indeed a curious attitude on the part of Europeans.

Indeed, whereas a person growing up in an Islamic country would hardly ask why they should follow the religion of the Prophet Mohammed and not Christ, modern Europeans, yes, post-Christian Europeans actually tend to defend the faith of others whilst rejecting their own!

The final layer to overcome when evangelizing Europeans is the matter of the Church. "Yes, I believe in God; I believe in Jesus. But why do you want me to go to Church? I can as well worship God at home."

To that, I will say that one does not have to belong to a church to be counted among Christians. Believers, especially young converts, generally need fellowship with other believers to grow in their faith; the church provides such an environment. So, I would personally recommend that, in particular, new converts to the faith seek Bible-believing churches to fellowship with.

* * *

The good news is that Almighty God has not abandoned Europe and, for that matter, the rest of the world. Every day, He sounds out His call: "Behold, I stand at the door and knock; whoever opens the door, I will come in and dine with them. Rev. 3:20 (KJV)

What then needs to be done?

Firstly, the unbelieving Europeans should humble his or her heart and accept that life was created by a Supernatural being, Almighty God.

Yes, the unbelieving European should free his or her mind from the erroneously engraved notion that life came from nothing. No, life did not come about out of mere accident or chance. Almighty God of Heaven and Earth created the Universe.

Next, Europe should understand that "God's ways are not ours". No, we cannot understand God's workings through our rational thinking. We would think 1 plus 1 is 2; well, the Divine does not make his calculations that way. His workings do not operate along the lines of humanity's logical thinking.

Indeed, the Lord works in mysterious ways. I can cite several instances from my life when I experienced the mysterious workings of Almighty God. For example, when I decided to follow the Lord in September 1978, I had just finished my GCE A Levels and looking to study in Ghana. The best I wished for myself was to attend medical school in my native Ghana. That was not to be. Through the mysterious leadings of the Lord, I ended up studying medicine in Germany!

This is no advertisement for my book, but those wishing to read how the Lord led me from my little village of Mpintimpi to medical school in Germany may read my book, *THE CALL THAT CHANGED MY LIFE* or the slightly abridged version *MEDICAL SCHOOL AT LAST.*

Europe was a privilege to be one of the continents to first receive the message of the Cross. As everyone agrees, Christianity led to a far-reaching transformation of European society. Having been massively blessed by the Gospel, why should Europe turn its back on it?

A fervent prayer for European Christian Revival

Before I end my presentation, I want to implore believers everywhere reading this piece to join me in prayer for European revival.

Yes, let us intercede before Almighty God on behalf of Europe. Let us lift our hands towards heaven in prayer for Europe.

Let us pray that the flame of the Church will be rekindled, yes, that Europe will come to worship Almighty God of Heaven and Earth.

Let us take authority in the Name of our Lord and Saviour Jesus Christ and declare in the Mighty Name of the Lord that as the Lord liveth, the flame of Christianity will continue to blaze over Europe; yes, that the Christian fire lit over two thousand years ago in Europe will not go out.

Yes, let us pray for a fresh wind of revival to blow across the continent to set free the captives of Satan.

Yes, the door of Christianity will remain open across Europe! No, Lucifer will not be able to shut the door of the Good News of the Cross—the comforting and liberating news that sets the sinner free.

Yes, for sure, Europe will continue to stand before Almighty God. Yes, the flame of Christianity will continue to lighten Europe today, tomorrow and forever.

In Jesus' Mighty Name, we pray! Amen!

CPSIA information can be obtained
at www.ICGtesting.com
Printed in the USA
BVHW050545140223
658474BV00023B/369